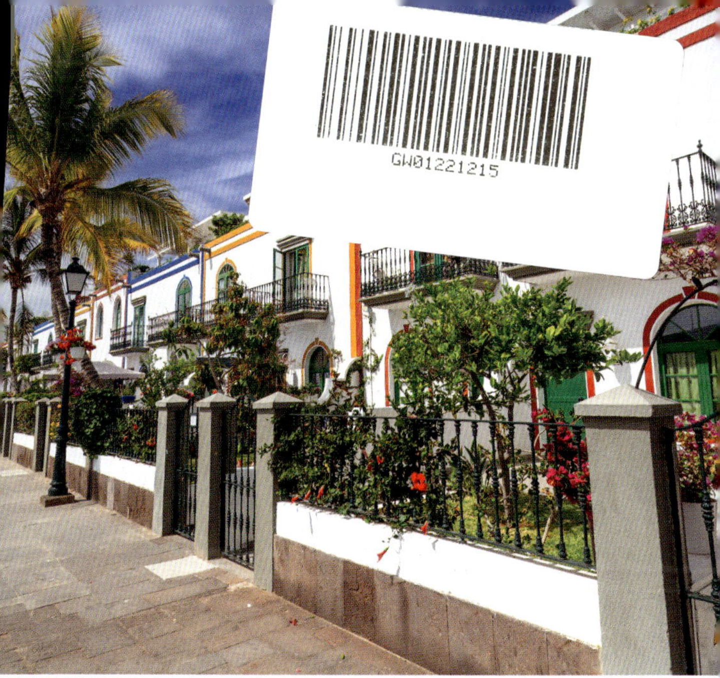

THE MINI ROUGH GUIDE TO
GRAN CANARIA

STARTS HERE

Tailor-made trips and unique adventures crafted by local experts

HOW ROUGHGUIDES.COM/TRIPS WORKS

STEP 1

Pick your dream destination, tell us what you want and submit an enquiry.

STEP 2

Fill in a short form to tell your local expert about your dream trip and preferences.

STEP 3

Our local expert will craft your tailor-made itinerary. You'll be able to tweak and refine it until you're completely satisfied.

STEP 4

Book online with ease, pack your bags and enjoy the trip! Our local expert will be on hand 24/7 while you're on the road.

PLAN AND BOOK YOUR TRIP AT ROUGHGUIDES.COM/TRIPS

HOW TO DOWNLOAD YOUR FREE EBOOK

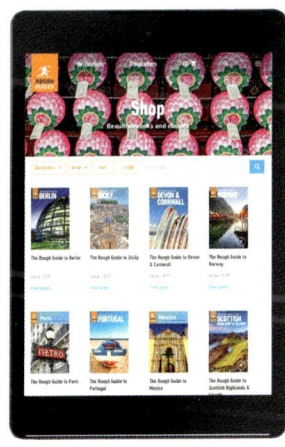

1. Visit **www.roughguides.com/free-ebook** or scan the **QR code** opposite

2. Enter the code **grancanaria578**

3. Follow the simple step-by-step instructions

For troubleshooting contact: mail@roughguides.com

10 THINGS NOT TO MISS

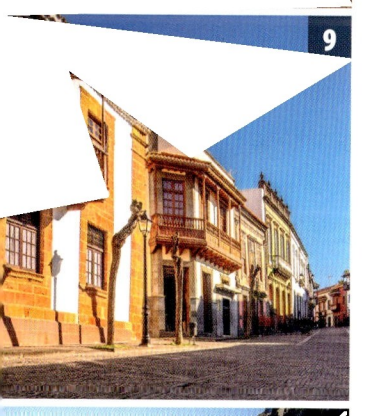

1. **ROQUE NUBLO**
   The towering monolith is a symbol of Gran Canaria. See page 76.

2. **PLAYA DE LAS CANTERAS**
   This lively city beach is popular with local people and tourists alike. See page 37.

3. **CRUZ DE TEJEDA**
   Marks one of the highest points on the island. See page 76.

4. **BARRANCO DE GUAYADEQUE**
   It is easy to drive through this beautiful valley. See page 45.

5. **MASPALOMAS**
   Its pristine dunes are like a desert by the sea. See page 51.

6. **PUERTO DE MOGÁN**
   One of the prettiest places on the island, this bougainvillea-draped village is a fine blend of tradition and tourism. See page 55.

7. **CENOBIO DE VALERÓN**
   The most impressive pre-Hispanic granary on the island. See page 68.

8. **CASA DE COLÓN**
   One of the most attractive traditional buildings in Las Palmas, it is claimed Columbus once stayed here. See page 33.

9. **TEROR**
   A sublime town with a long, storied history. See page 72.

10. **MIRADOR DEL BALCÓN**
    Enjoy a break from the demanding west coast road at this stunning viewpoint. See page 61.

A PERFECT DAY

9am

Breakfast. Kick off the day with a leisurely breakfast beneath the trees at a table outside the pretty little Art Nouveau kiosk café in Parque San Telmo (see page 28).

10am

City vistas. For a panoramic view of the city, take the lift that whizzes you up to the rooftop of the twin-towered Catedral de Santa Ana. When you've taken in the sublime vistas, visit the cathedral itself to enjoy the cool, quiet peace of the delightful cloister.

11am

Casa de Colón. Visit the butter-hued Casa de Colón to admire the ornate latticed balconies and the replica of a cabin from one of Columbus's ships.

Noon

Pueblo Canario. Take a bus or taxi to leafy Parque Doramas to admire the splendour of the *Hotel Santa Catalina* and visit the Pueblo Canario, a beautifully designed complex of traditional island buildings and a museum that pays homage to artist Néstor Martín-Fernández de la Torre, one of the brothers behind the design.

1.30pm

Lunch. Hop in another taxi to Parque Santa Catalina, where elderly men play chess beneath the palms, and horse-drawn carriages await passengers. After wandering through the leafy grounds, stop for a light lunch at *Gambrinus* (tel: 928 223 321) on Calle Secretario Artiles. It's a *cerveceria* (brewery), which means the beer will be good.

IN **LAS PALMAS**

3pm

Museo Elder. If you're travelling with children, the Museo Elder is a must-visit. Even if you are not, you will be fascinated by this innovative science and technology museum, set in a building that belonged to the Elder Dempster Shipping Line in the days when Britain colonized the island.

4.30pm

Playa de las Canteras. Head across the narrow neck of the peninsula to Playa de las Canteras for a swim in the bathwater-warm shallow water, protected by a reef called La Barra. Soak up some sun on the sands, then stroll along the lively promenade until you reach the prestigious Auditorio Alfredo Kraus, home to the Las Palmas Philharmonic Orchestra.

7pm

Aperitif time. When you are ready to head out for the evening, make your way to Plazoleta de Cairasco where you can check out which exhibitions are on at the cultural centre known as CICCA. Once you have got your art fix, linger over an aperitif in the elegant square while you watch the sun go down.

8.30pm

Dinner. It's not too far to walk to *Deliciosa Marta* (see page 106), in Calle Pérez Galdós, an excellent restaurant serving some of the finest food in town. And if you still have energy to burn, head to *La Azotea de Benito* in Plaza Hurtado del Mendoza, a cool rooftop bar where the party continues late into the night.

CONTENTS

OVERVIEW — 10

HISTORY AND CULTURE — 15

OUT AND ABOUT — 27

Las Palmas — 27
Triana 28, Vegueta 30, Three Vegueta Museums 32, Parque Doramas and the Pueblo Canario 34, Parque Santa Catalina 35, Around the port 36, Playa de las Canteras 37, La Isleta and around 38

The East — 40
Jardín Canario 40, Caldera de Bandama 42, Telde 43, Cuatro Puertas 44, Ingenio 44, Barranco de Guayadeque 45, Agüimes 47, Arinaga 48

The Southern Resorts — 48
San Agustín 49, Playa del Inglés 49, Maspalomas 51, Inland excursions 53, Puerto Rico 54, Puerto de Mogán 55, Mogán 57

Going West — 57
Mountain route 57, San Nicolás de Tolentino 59, Puerto de la Aldea 60, Coastal road 61, Puerto de las Nieves 62, Agaete 64

The North — 65
Gáldar 66, Sardina 67, Santa María de Guía 68, Cenobio de Valerón 68, Moya 68, Arucas 70, Firgas and the Finca de Osorio 71, Teror 72

The Central Peaks — 74
Cruz de Tejeda 76, Artenara 77, Pinar de Tamadaba 77, Barranco de Fataga 78, Pico de las Nieves and Roque Bentaiga 79, Fortaleza Grande and Santa Lucía 81

THINGS TO DO 83

Sports 83
Shopping 90
Nightlife 93
Children's Gran Canaria 94

FOOD AND DRINK 97

WHERE TO STAY 133

INDEX 143

HIGHLIGHTS

British interests 20
Important dates 25
Famous son 29
Cave dwellers 46
The Count's vision 52
Bringing down the branches 63
Caminos reales 80
Ancient sports 87
What's on 96

OVERVIEW

The Canary Islands have always been regarded as a bridge between continents. They were the last stopping-off point for Columbus on his journey of discovery in 1492, when emergency repairs were done in Las Palmas to one of his three ships. During the sixteenth and seventeenth centuries, the islands were important trading centres through which passed much of the profitable sea traffic between Spain and the Americas. Latin American influences are still visible, in the food and the language, while the architecture reminds us that these were Spanish colonies at a time when the peninsula was at its most wealthy and powerful.

The archipelago lies in the Atlantic Ocean, some 1100km (700 miles) southwest of mainland Spain and comprises the islands of Gran Canaria, Lanzarote and Fuerteventura to the east, and Tenerife, La Gomera, La Palma and El Hierro to the west. Gran Canaria, the third-largest island, is around 195km (120 miles) from the African mainland, on a level with southern Morocco, and covers an area of 1532 sq km (592 sq miles).

A LAND OF EXTREMES

Gran Canaria was formed some 16 million years ago by volcanic activity beneath the Atlantic, at a point where continental drift made the ocean bed particularly unstable. The central mountain massif was once a volcano, and the gorges *(barrancos)* radiating from it were formed by the subsequent process of erosion. Although the island is small, it is extremely diverse. The eastern side is lush and fertile; the north and west bleak and barren; while the expanse of white-sand dunes in the south, barely populated until the 1960s, is now the island's holiday playground. Coastal roads in the west are winding and vertiginous, with stunning views, while away from the coast, all roads lead upwards. The highest point is the Pico de las Nieves – Peak of the Snows – at 1949m (6394ft).

Vegetation on Gran Canaria is as varied as the landscape. The fire-resistant Canary pine *(Pinus canariensis)* rules over the mountainous zone, while a pink rock rose *(Cistus symphytifolius)* clusters around its feet, and varieties of thyme, sage and broom scent the air. The Canary Island spurge *(Euphorbia canariensis)* sur-

vives well in the dry southern region, as does tajinaste *(Echium decaisnei)*, a kind of borage, and the Cardon cactus *(Pachycereus pringlei)*, while southern valleys support verdant groves of date palms *(Phoenix canariensis)*. Prickly pear *(Opuntia ficus indica)* is seen all over the northern and central areas; imported from Mexico in the sixteenth century, it was used to cultivate the cochineal beetle. The most unusual flora is the dragon tree *(Dracaena draco)*, which took its name from its red resin known as dragon's blood; this ancient survivor is mostly seen in botanical gardens. The plants you spot immediately – brilliant bougainvillaea, hibiscus and poinsettia, clambering over walls and brightening parks and gardens – are not indigenous but were brought to the islands from subtropical parts and have flourished in the equable climate.

Island birds include the native blue chaffinch *(pinzón* in Spanish); greenfinches (not indigenous but very happy here); greater-spotted woodpeckers in the pine forests; the shy Canary chat; and canaries. These are not the bright yellow we are accustomed to seeing, but little dun-hued creatures that changed colour when they were caged and their breeding controlled. However, the wild ones sing as sweetly as their caged cousins.

Gran Canaria has year-round sunshine – some 300 days a year in the south. A strange grey haze called the *panza de burro* – donkey's belly – sometimes shrouds the north. Winter temperatures average 22–24°C (72–75°F), summer sees the mercury hover around 26–28°C (79–82°F), though it often nudges over 30°C (86°F). High season is November to April, but July and August are also popular with Spanish visitors and, despite the heat, with English and German families taking advantage of long school holidays.

THE PEOPLE OF GRAN CANARIA

Gran Canaria is part of the Spanish Autonomous Region of the Canary Islands. The population numbers 847,000, of whom over 383,000 live in the capital, Las Palmas. They are, on the whole, relaxed, open-minded people, but keen to stress that they are *canarios*, first and foremost. Islanders refer to mainland Spaniards as *'los peninsulares'*.

Spanish *(castellano)* is the language of the islands. However, there are differences from the peninsula, many of which reflect the two-way traffic between the Canaries and Latin America. Final consonants are swallowed and 'z' is pronounced 's', as in the Americas, rather than the lisped 'th' of mainland Spain. A number of Latino words have been borrowed, too: a bus is a *guagua* and potatoes are *papas*. The strong English influence on the islands has also left some linguistic traces: a cake is a *queque*, and a traditional Canarian knife is a *naife*.

There is a large expatriate population – chiefly English and German – many of whom came for holidays and either bought retirement homes or opened bars or restaurants. The official religion is Catholic, although Anglican, Muslim, Mormon and other religions have a presence.

Most of the traditional festivals on the island have religious origins. The wild pre-Lent carnival stands out for its sheer exuberance – a time of elaborate parades, costumes and riotous behaviour – but there are other fascinating ones, including the Virgen del Carmen Festival, when the patron saint of the sea is honoured in ports across the island; the Bajada de las Ramas in Puerto de las Nieves; and the hugely popular mix of religious and secular celebrations for the Virgen del Pino in Teror.

Carnival cheer

Carnival began as a religious event, a last celebration before the lean days of Lent, and developed into a riotous affair, with lavish processions and costumed balls. Carnival takes place throughout the Catholic world and the major ones in Gran Canaria and Tenerife are usually staggered so they do not take place at exactly the same time.

ECONOMY AND ENVIRONMENT

Traditionally, the island's economy has been dependent on agriculture, from sugar cane in the sixteenth century to cochineal, bananas and tomatoes. The principal source of employment today is in the service sector, of which tourism is a major part. EU funds have been used to strengthen the island infrastructure – roads, airports and hospitals.

There are plans for a rail line between Las Palmas and Playa del Inglés, but at the time of writing work has not yet started. The island suffers from a water shortage, a problem intensified by the strain that overtourism can place on the system, but this has been partly overcome by the creation of desalination plants, some fuelled by wind power.

In an attempt to break away from the 'sun, sand and sangria' image of the islands, a *turismo rural* initiative has reimagined

Tejeda, at the foot of Roque Nublo

traditional buildings as rural hotels in areas of great natural beauty, providing a peaceful base for walkers and nature lovers.

REASONS TO VISIT

Although many people visit Gran Canaria for its sun-bleached beaches, there is so much more to the island. Las Palmas is an enchanting capital city with a vibrant energy. There are two theatres, a cultural centre with a varied programme, excellent restaurants, a lively nightlife, and a clutch of good museums. The central mountainous region of the island, crowned by the Pico de las Nieves, offers great walking and climbing opportunities, while the northern towns of Arucas and Teror have delightful historic centres with traditional architecture. The *barrancos* (gorges) are lush with tropical vegetation. The south is ideal for boating and watersports, with craft and equipment available for hire; and, a short distance from the brash resorts, the vast and empty dunes of Maspalomas feel like a desert by the sea.

HISTORY AND CULTURE

Much of the Canary Islands' history is tied up with that of the Spanish mainland. As a vital point for trade with the Americas, Gran Canaria briefly shared in the prosperity of Spain's Golden Age, although it suffered economic decline thereafter. And in the late twentieth century, the islands, along with Spain, became part of the European Union. But long before the Spaniards ever set foot here, there was a flourishing civilization.

LAND OF THE BRAVE

Tamarán – Land of the Brave – was the proud name given to Gran Canaria by the Guanches, the pre-Hispanic people of the islands.

No one is quite sure of the origins of the Guanches. Some historians and scientists think they were related to the Canarii people, who lived on the Saharan side of the Atlas Mountains. The few fragments of writing that can be reconstructed are similar to scripts used by the ancient Amazigh (Berber) people, and some Canarian place names are similar too. But as far as can be deduced, the Guanches had no boats, so how they crossed from the African coast remains a mystery.

Nonetheless, archeological evidence has revealed much about the culture of these original islanders. Language and social structure varied from island to island. On Gran Canaria, the rulers were called *guanartemes* and shared some of their power with a *faycan*, who combined the role of judge and priest. Next on the social ladder came the aristocracy, the *guayres*.

The Guanches were a settled, agricultural people, who lived in groups of caves. *Gofio,* toasted flour originally made from barley, was the staple of their diet, but they also ate a variety of root vegetables, wild fruits and berries. Pigs, sheep and goats provided meat as well as the materials for shelters, containers and clothes, and milk also came from sheep and goats. Fish formed a part of their diet, even when they had to travel some distance down to the coast to find it.

The Guanches did not have the wheel, they knew nothing of metalworking and did not use bows and arrows. Their domestic implements were made from stone and bone or from obsidian, a black, volcanic glass. Porous lava was made into millstones and mortars. Their vessels and containers were made from pottery, wood, leather and woven cane. They mummified their dead and buried them in caves or stone-lined graves, and it is evidence from mummies so far unearthed that has led scientists to place the original islanders' ethnic origins in northwest Africa. The Museo Canario exhibits mummies and skulls in its collection, along with domestic items, remarkably well preserved in the dry climate.

THE CONQUERORS ARRIVE

The first conquering force, in 1403, was led by a Norman lord, Jean de Béthencourt, and funded by the king of Castile, but he failed to take the two main prizes – Gran Canaria and Tenerife. It wasn't until 1478 that another attempt was made, under the aegis of the Catholic Monarchs – Ferdinand and Isabella – of a newly united Spain. As the

force was undermanned and the Indigenous people put up a fight, it took several years to colonize Gran Canaria. Two events contributed to the islanders' downfall: Pedro de Vera arrived as military governor in 1480, and is said to have killed one of the most powerful Guanche Chiefs, Doramas, with his own hands on the Montaña de Arucas. This coup, along with the capture and conversion two years later of Chief Tenesor Semidan, contributed to the conquest of the Guanche people, but not before many of them had been killed, starved to death or died by ritual suicide.

De Vera remained governor for 10 years, during which time he had many of the local population deported or enslaved. This, together with an influx of European farmers and entrepreneurs, plus two severe outbreaks of plague, meant that within half a century the Indigenous population was outnumbered. Those who survived had been forcibly converted to Catholicism and many had intermarried with the incomers.

PROSPERITY AND DECLINE

Because of their location, the Canary Islands became a 'successful' example for future Spanish colonization strategies in the Americas. These revolved around slavery and sugar cane, both of which were introduced to the Americas from the Canaries. The sugar boom on the Canaries only lasted until the mid-sixteenth century, when competition from Brazil and the Caribbean became too strong. While Tenerife was able to switch to a lucrative wine industry, conditions on Gran Canaria were unsuitable for viniculture and the island became something of a poor relation, locked in fierce rivalry with its flourishing sibling. Tenerife came out on top as the residence of the Captain-General and location of the first university.

The problems Gran Canaria suffered during the sixteenth and seventeenth centuries were intensified by the fact that the island and her ships were frequently attacked by pirates. The worst outrage was in 1599, when Dutch buccaneer Pieter van der Does sacked and burned Las Palmas. Gran Canaria began to assert its independence – from Tenerife and mainland Spain – in 1808 when the Napoleonic Wars destroyed Tenerife's wine trade. A junta was formed in Las Palmas, calling for 'a patriotic government, independent of the peninsula', but it was unsuccessful.

Not until the 1860s did the island's fortunes begin to recover, with the introduction of cochineal, the red dye produced from a beetle of the same name that feeds on cacti. The boom was

> **Pirate attack**
>
> The Bishop's Palace in Las Palmas was one notable victim of Dutch pirate Pieter van der Does' attack; another was Catedral de Santa Ana. In a display case in the cathedral today there is a splendid bell, a gift from the Asociación Nederlandesa-Canaria in 1999, 500 years after the privateer destroyed the original.

Gran Canaria suffered many pirate attacks in the seventeenth century

short-lived, as the invention of cheaply produced aniline dyes brought a virtual end to the industry. Poverty and unemployment forced many islanders to emigrate to the Americas, mainly Cuba and Venezuela.

It was only in the 1880s that things really began to get better, largely due to Fernando León y Castillo, a local politician who became foreign minister in the Spanish government. With the collaboration of his brother, Juan, an engineer, he embarked on a project to transform Las Palmas into the major port on the island. Within about six years, the Puerto de la Luz was dealing with most of the steamship trade that passed through the archipelago.

WAR AND RECOVERY

The last of the briefly successful monocultures was bananas, introduced by the British in the late nineteenth century. But World War I had a disastrous effect on the trade, creating more poverty and more emigration. After Cuba won freedom from Spain in 1898, there were calls for Canarian independence, but most people simply wanted the division of the archipelago into two separate provinces. Formalization of this came in 1927 but no new economic solutions had been found when the three-year Spanish Civil War

BRITISH INTERESTS

There is a street in Las Palmas called Alfredo Jones, another called Tomás Miller, and the science museum is the Museo Elder. They were named after three of the British businessmen who had the most influence on Las Palmas in the nineteenth and early twentieth centuries. There was a fourth – James Swanton – who seems to have been overlooked when street names were doled out. British influence on the island was far-reaching. Swanton and his young cousin, Thomas Miller, ran an import–export business, started in the 1820s. It flourished at the height of the cochineal boom. When aniline dyes killed demand, Miller began importing coal from Cardiff. The Santa Catalina jetty in the new port was financed by a second generation of Millers and Swantons; major shipping lines with offices in the port were British-owned – one was the Elder Dempster Line, in whose premises the Museo Elder is housed; and the water, electricity and telephone services were all set up by Englishmen. Sir Alfred Jones never lived on the island, but he founded the Grand Canary Coaling Company and financed the construction of the *Hotel Santa Catalina*. These wealthy businessmen established *Club Inglés* (British Club; still in Calle León y Castillo) and founded the first golf club. They built houses in the leafy Ciudad Jardín (Garden City) in Las Palmas and on the hills outside, in Tafira and Santa Brígida, still regarded as desirable places to live. For several decades at least, Gran Canaria was an informal colony of the British Empire.

Franco and his men at a secret meeting in Tenerife just before his coup

began in 1936, initiated by Francisco Franco, military governor of the Canary Islands. He spent the last night before launching his coup in the *Hotel Madrid* in Las Palmas.

After the civil war and World War II, the Canaries, like the rest of Spain, suffered from isolation and economic hardship. Things improved a little in the 1950s, when Spain was once more recognized by the international community, but it was the advent of tourism in the following decade that really turned the tide. Franco remained in power until his death in 1975, when his authoritarian regime was replaced by a democratic government. The new Spanish Constitution of 1978 created the Autonomous Region of the Canary Islands – now one of seventeen such regions. The archipelago is not completely separate from Spain but the island government, the Cabildo Insular, does have a great deal of freedom.

The islands have enjoyed considerable commercial freedom and tax exemptions ever since the nineteenth century, but when Spain became a full member of the European Union, fiscal changes had to be introduced. To protect trade and industry, the Puerto de la Luz and the industrial area round Arinaga were confirmed as a Free Trade Zone, governed by a local consortium.

The economy is not unhealthy, but it does need some support. The agricultural sector finds it difficult to compete in the wider market. Until the end of 1995, Spain guaranteed a market for Gran Canaria's bananas but since then, despite EU subsidies, the industry has plummeted. Production costs are high, and bananas need a lot of water – a scarce commodity. The island is a major supplier of tomatoes for the European market, but countries with lower labour costs, such as Morocco, have been able to undercut the Canarian growers. The only real money-spinner is tourism.

TOURISM AND THE ENVIRONMENT

The creation of the resorts of San Agustín, Playa del Inglés and Maspalomas in the 1960s, catering to sun-seeking northern Europeans, changed the face of Gran Canaria. This, together with the opening of Gando international airport in 1974, made tourism the main industry. The economy skyrocketed and islanders gained employment, for most of the year at least, but inevitably there were detrimental effects on the environment. Hotels, swimming pools and golf courses are problematic for an island with a water shortage. Heavy traffic took its toll on the roads. And the island's reputation as a holiday destination suffered, too, from the alcohol-fuelled antics of some tourists.

For ecological and economic reasons, the Cabildo Insular has made huge efforts to diversify the tourist industry and protect the environment. Many areas have been designated natural parks and nature reserves; in fact, over 66,000 hectares (154,000 acres), some 40 percent of the island, is protected to some degree. Active environmental groups exert a steadying influence.

WIND, WATER AND FIRE

Water on the island is not only in short supply but, until relatively recently, was also in the hands of private suppliers. This has always been a contentious issue and, in the south, it has been taken out of private hands and is run by a franchise called Canaragua. Water shortages have been alleviated to some extent by desalination plants – there are two huge ones run by a private company, Acciona Agua. Wind power has been introduced to keep costs down, and the gigantic wind farm at Pozo Izquierdo on the gusty east coast is the foremost example of this.

In 2007, the island suffered from its worst forest fires in over fifty years. Low humidity, high temperatures and strong winds contributed to the devastation that led to the evacuation of over 5000 people from their homes. Around 20,000 hectares (50,000 acres) of ground was burnt, particularly in the mountains around Mogán. Fortunately, no lives were lost. Two years later, another wildfire in

the south of the island damaged some 25,000 hectares (62,000 acres) and forced a mass evacuation, but the region recovered well.

A GENTLER IMAGE

Gran Canaria's tourist industry suffered less than that of the rest of Spain during the economic downturn of the early twenty-first century, and visitor numbers have risen dramatically in recent years. The industry has been given a new direction, with less emphasis on sun, sea and sand, and more on environmentally conscious aspects of the island. EU funds have helped in the promotion of the *turismo rural* initiative – a strategy that helps to convert traditional buildings into country hotels.

The opening up of the *caminos reales* (royal paths) in Gran Canaria's interior is part of a drive to attract walkers and cyclists. There has also been a resurgence of interest in the island's pre-Hispanic past and cultural heritage. In Gáldar, one of the two ancient capitals, which calls itself the Ciudad de los Guanartemes (City of Rulers), most of the streets have Indigenous names, and the state-of-the-art Cueva Pintada Archaeological Museum traces the island's long history. An increasing number of children are being given Guanche names, such as Tamara or Tenesor, and a favoured name for bars and restaurants is Tagoror, which means a place of assembly. Perhaps this is all part of a move to establish a new sense of island identity, while remaining very much a part of Europe.

IMPORTANT DATES

c. 1st–2nd centuries BC Guanche settlements in Canary Islands.
AD1477–83 Spanish force lands on the island and subdues Guanches.
1492 Columbus briefly stops at Las Palmas before sailing to America.
c. 1500 Sugar cane introduced and enslaved Africans imported. From 1554, the sugar industry declines.
1700–1950 Poverty forces widespread emigration to Latin America.
1852 Isabella II declares the Canary Islands a Free Trade Zone.
1890 The British introduce bananas as a monoculture.
1911 Self-administration council – Cabildo Insular – introduced.
1927 The Canary Islands are divided into two provinces. Las Palmas de Gran Canaria becomes capital of the eastern province.
1936 Franco, military governor of the Canary Islands, initiates the three-year Spanish Civil War.
1956 The first charter plane lands on Gran Canaria. Tourism rapidly develops into the most important industry.
1974 Gando international airport opens.
1978–82 New Spanish Constitution joins the two island provinces to form the Autonomous Region of the Canary Islands.
1986 Spain joins the EU and negotiates a special status for the Canaries.
1995 Islands integrated into the EU but retain important tax privileges.
2002 The euro becomes the national currency.
2005 Islands hit by Tropical Storm Delta, causing severe damage.
2007 Summer fires devastate the Mogán region.
2009 More fires in Mogán cause damage but the area quickly recovers.
2010–11 Gran Canaria (and Tenerife) buck the trend by attracting greater numbers of tourists despite the economic downturn.
2014 A record number of foreign tourists (3.13 million) visit Gran Canaria. Several oil spills affect beaches in the southern part of the island.
2020 Covid-19 pandemic hits Gran Canaria; travel restrictions leave beaches and hotels empty and bring businesses to the brink of collapse.
2022 Tourism starts to recover as Covid-19 restrictions are lifted.
2022–23 The Canary Islands bustle once again with visitors.

OUT AND ABOUT

Gran Canaria is not a huge island but what it lacks in size, it makes up for in diversity. You only have to travel the short distance south from capital city Las Palmas to the dry dunes of Maspalomas, then head northwest to explore the lush Barranco de Agaete, scale the mountainous central heights, or spend a peaceful day in one of the coastal fishing ports, and you will feel as though you have visited a small continent.

LAS PALMAS

Las Palmas ❶, the sprawling capital of Gran Canaria, has a population of over 400,000 people, nearly 80 percent of whom make their living in the service industries. The city is divided into several distinct enclaves. To the south is the Unesco-listed historical centre, Vegueta, which is separated by a busy dual carriageway from Triana, an attractive old shopping quarter peppered with cafés and Art Nouveau buildings. The traffic-filled Avenida Marítima and noisy Calle León y Castillo lead to the next points of interest: lush Parque Doramas and the Muelle Deportivo yacht harbour. A further busy stretch, either following the sea or on a parallel road inland, marches to the huge Puerto de la Luz and lively Parque Santa Catalina. From here, a grid of streets links the city and the beach, Playa de las Canteras, the island's original holiday resort.

Between these points are the busy commercial streets around Avenida Mesa y López and Ciudad Jardín, where flowers blossom in walled gardens and flags fly above government buildings. At the far northern tip is La Isleta, a working-class district with a clutch of excellent fish restaurants; up on the hills behind is the Ciudad Alta where many of the capital's citizens live and work.

TRIANA

Whether you come straight from the airport or travel on a bus trip from the south, you are likely to arrive at **Parque San Telmo A**, for this is the site of one of the city's two bus terminals and the place where taxis wait to ferry passengers to other parts of town. There's a children's playground in the square and a pretty little chapel, the Ermita de San Telmo, its unassuming whitewashed facade concealing ornate and gilded interiors. Opposite, an Art Nouveau kiosk, decorated with gleaming tiles, serves drinks to patrons at tables beneath towering *fisco* trees; and the Quiosco de la Música bandstand stages regular concerts. At the back of the square, a plaque on a military building informs that here, on 18 July 1936, Franco announced the coup that initiated the Spanish Civil War.

To the left of the square, the pedestrianized **Calle Mayor de Triana** is flanked by a string of attractive facades – some colonial in style, others Art Nouveau – fronting a medley of shops, from a tiny fabric store and old-fashioned tobacconists to well-known high street brands. To the right, the narrow, pretty streets are reminiscent of the Triana district in Seville from which this area took its name, and are lined by smart boutiques and a sprinkling of antiques and gift shops. The Librería del Cabildo Insular (www.libreriadelcabildo.com) on the corner of Cano and Travieso, is stocked with a wide choice of books and maps on the islands.

Calle Cano is also the place to find the **Casa-Museo Pérez Galdós** B (www.casamuseoperezgaldos.com; Tues–Sun 10am–6pm; guided tours on the hour). The building where Spanish novelist Benito Pérez Galdós was born in 1843 (see box, below) is a splendid example of Canarian architecture, built around a courtyard and decorated with portraits and furniture from his houses in Madrid and Santander, many of which he designed and created himself. Further south on Calle Alfonso XIII is the beautiful blue building of the **Casa Africa**, (exhibitions Mon–Fri 10am–6.30pm; www.casafrica.es), which promotes African culture and celebrates relations between Europe, Africa and South America.

Close by is a little jewel of a square, the **Plazoleta de Cairasco**. The *Hotel Madrid*, one of the oldest in the city, serves meals and drinks at outdoor tables beneath the palms till late at night. At the north end, the splendid **Gabinete Literario**, floodlit after dark, is an Art Nouveau treasure and designated a 'Monumento Histórico Artistico'. Once a theatre, it is now home to a literary society (www.

FAMOUS SON

Benito Pérez Galdós (1843–1920) is widely regarded as one of the greatest Spanish novelists and playwrights, and many believe he would have received the Nobel Prize for Literature had it not been for his unpopular political views. His books and plays offer an inside view of Spanish life, and he was unusual in that he did not restrict himself to the world of just one social class. Born in Las Palmas, he spent much of his life in Madrid and Santander, where he became increasingly involved with politics. A staunch republican, he was elected as a senator for Madrid in 1910, and for Las Palmas when he returned in 1914. His greatest play, *Electra*, received its premier in the theatre named after him in Triana (www.teatroperezgaldos.es).

gabineteliterario.com), and also houses a restaurant-café with comfortable chairs on a shady terrace.

To the side of the little plaza runs the **Alameda de Colón**, at the north end of which, near a bust of Columbus, is the whitewashed, colonial-style **Iglesia de San Francisco**. Destroyed in the fire of 1599, following Dutch pirate Pieter van der Does' attack, it was rebuilt in the seventeenth century, then became a parochial church after the monks were ejected (as they were throughout Spain in 1821). At the south end of the *alameda* (tree-lined avenue), in an imposing building with stone-framed doorways, is a cultural centre, known by the acronym **CICCA**, where La Caja de las Canarias, a munificent savings bank, funds exhibitions, films, music and theatrical performances.

You are close now to the major highway (Calle Juan de Quesada) that separates Triana from Vegueta, but before you cross there's another attractive square to swing by. It is officially called Hurtado de Mendoza, after an early twentieth-century painter, but usually known as **Las Ranas**, or The Frogs, because the long pool that runs down the centre is fed by two spouting amphibians.

A cluster of bars and street food spots can be found around Frogs Square and Monopol Boulevard, and the area is always buzzing with a young crowd at night. Nearby is an imposing library building, also frequented by students from the university a short distance up the highway; there is some student accommodation in Triana.

VEGUETA

The historic centre of Las Palmas has a character all of its own. This was once the aristocratic quarter, and its cobbled streets are lined with colonial buildings with intricately carved balconies and palm-filled interior courtyards, glimpsed when their huge, polished doors are ajar.

Twin-towered Catedral de Santa Ana

At its heart, in **Plaza de Santa Ana** ©, is the twin-towered **Catedral de Santa Ana** (Mon–Sat 10am–4.30pm; www.catedral-santaana.com; access only through Diocesan Museum). Started in 1497, it wasn't completed until the twentieth century and is a glorious mishmash of architectural styles – Gothic, Renaissance and Neoclassical. Intricate details on the facade and many of the statues inside are the work of the Canary Island sculptor, José Luján Pérez (1756–1815).

The adjoining **Museo Diocesano de Arte Sacro** (hours as above; entrance in Calle Espíritu Santo) has a lovely cloister, the Patio de los Naranjos (Orange Trees). Among the sacred paintings and artefacts on display is an impressive modern series, *Stations of the Cross*, by local artist Jesús Arencibia. If you don't want to visit the museum and cathedral, you could take the modern lift (same hours; separate charge), which will whisk you to the top of one of the towers for a great view over the city.

Among the magnificent buildings in the plaza, the **Palacio Regental** may be the star. It is largely seventeenth century, although the facade dates from 1867. The Canarian balcony is older, as is the huge and splendid doorway, above which is the coat of arms of the kingdoms of León and Castile. Little remains of the adjoining **Palacio Episcopal** (Bishop's Palace) except an ornate single-storey facade. It was a victim of the fire of 1599, when Dutch privateer Pieter van der Does destroyed most of the town (see page 18).

Huge bronze dogs – the island's heraldic animal – guard the cathedral, and at the other end of the palm-lined square is the elegant nineteenth-century building housing the **Casas Consistoriales** (Offices of Island Government).

Beyond the square is the little Plaza Espíritu Santo with its unusual domed fountain in the centre. From here, Calle Dr Chil leads to the Museo Canario. This is a street of splendid houses with carved wooden balconies and intriguing, shady courtyards, most of which are now the homes and offices of lawyers.

The Vegueta food market on Calle Medizábel (Mon–Sat 6.30am–2pm) sells fruit and vegetables as well as fresh fish, local cured meats and pungent cheeses. There are good local tascas and bars dotted throughout the surrounding streets.

THREE VEGUETA MUSEUMS

The first of three Vegueta museums that deserve attention is the **Museo Canario** O (www.elmuseocanario.com; Mon–Fri 10am–8pm, Sat–Sun 10am–2pm) on Calle Dr Verneau. It houses the Canary Islands' largest collection of pre-Hispanic objects – pottery, tools, mummies and skeletons, and dozens of skulls, lined up in glass cases like macabre ornaments. Here, you will see the ochre-coloured figure of the Idolo de Tara, a fertility goddess, copies of which are on sale in souvenir shops all over the island. There are

also scale models of Guanche dwellings and a replica of the Cueva Pintada in Gáldar (see page 67). Further east, at Ramón y Cajal 1, in a beautifully refurbished eighteenth-century former hospital, is the San Martín Centro de la Cultura Contemporánea (www.sanmartincontemporaneo.com; Tues–Sat 10am–9pm, Sun 10am–2pm), a contemporary art gallery and concert hall.

The **Casa de Colón** ❸ (www.casadecolon.com; Mon–Sat 10am–6pm, Sat 10am–3pm) is an endearing little museum, with ornate doorways and beautiful latticed balconies. Colón is the Spanish name for Columbus, and it is claimed, with no supporting evidence, that he stayed here while one of his ships was being repaired. The thirteen exhibition rooms and three large patios feature a replica of the cabin of *La Niña*, one of Columbus's fleet, nautical maps and charts, and a collection of pre-Columbian artefacts from Ecuador and Mexico. The house was the birthplace, in 1927, of the operatic tenor Alfredo Kraus.

> **Columbus's prayer**
>
> A plaque on the wall of San Antonio Abad, the tiny chapel next to the Casa de Colón, claims that the explorer stopped to pray on this spot before setting off on his voyage of discovery.

The **Centro Atlántico de Arte Moderno** (CAAM; caam.net; Tues-Sat 10am-9pm, Sun 10am-2pm) is worth visiting mainly because it is a wonderful exhibition space – white walls, marble stairs and acres of glass, concealed behind a traditional facade. It has a good reputation as an educational and cultural centre, but visitors may find its changing exhibitions are generally of less interest than the building itself.

PARQUE DORAMAS AND THE PUEBLO CANARIO

Leave the old town now and hop on a bus (from Teatro Pérez Galdós on the Triana side of the highway, or from Parque San Telmo) to **Parque Doramas**, set in a prosperous part of town known as the Ciudad Jardín. Amid tropical greenery in front of the smart **Hotel Santa Catalina**, a large statue dedicated to the vanquished Chief Doramas shows Guanche people leaping from a rocky fountain.

To the left of the hotel is the **Pueblo Canario** ❼, a little complex of traditional island buildings with café tables in a central plaza. This Canarian village was designed in the 1930s by brothers Néstor and Miguel Fernández de la Torre, to try to spike the interest of early tourists in island ways. Costumed folk dancing displays are held in the central square here every Sunday (11am–noon; free). The **Museo Néstor** (closed for restoration until further notice), dedicated to the better known of the brothers, is part of the complex. Born in Las Palmas, Néstor (1887–1938), always known simply by his first name, spent much of his life in Paris, Madrid and Barcelona, where he became famous for his sensuous paintings and imaginative stage designs. He returned to the island in later

PARQUE SANTA CATALINA   35

life with a heightened awareness of his roots and painted two series of works, *Atlantic Poem* and *Visiones de Gran Canaria* – both can be seen in the museum. There are also rooms dedicated to Canarian music and architecture.

Opposite the park is the Club Natación Metropol swimming and sports club (www.cnmetropole.com). Beside it, an underpass leads below the Avenida Marítima to the **Muelle Deportivo G**, the yacht harbour, from where transatlantic yachtsmen set out, and visitors can take catamaran trips. The waterfront promenade is lined with restaurants, cafés and shops, protected from the traffic on the road above. Adjoining the harbour area is the smart Real Club Náutico (www.rcngc.com) beside the Playa de Alcaravaneras, a stretch of beach mostly frequented by local families, so busiest at weekends.

PARQUE SANTA CATALINA

If you want to do any shopping, head inland along broad Calle Mesa y López, where most of the big stores are found, including a branch of Spain's largest department store, *El Corte Inglés*. Otherwise, it's not far to the next point of interest, **Parque Santa Catalina H**. Although dotted with palm trees and vivid flowerbeds, this, like San Telmo, is more of a square than a park, but much bigger and busier. There is always a sense of

activity here, with visitors and local people chatting at outdoor cafés; crowds of elderly men playing chess, dominos and cards in the shade of awnings; and local vendors calling to attract attention. Here, you can get local information from a small kiosk, board one of the open-topped hop-on-hop-off *guagua turística* buses for a spot of sightseeing, or book tickets in the Fred Olsen office for the ferry to Tenerife. The company runs a free bus to Agaete to connect with the ferries.

AROUND THE PORT

On the port side of the park is the striking **Museo Elder** (www.museoelder.org; Tues–Thurs 9.30am–7.30pm, Fri–Sun 10am–8pm), a wonderful science and technology museum housed in a building that belonged to the Elder Dempster Shipping Line. There are lots of interactive exhibits to amuse children, as well as an industrial robot spot-welding a car, a model of Foucault's pendulum, an incubator where patient visitors can watch chicks hatching from eggs, and an IMAX cinema.

A landscaped pedestrian area leads from the museum to the **Muelle Santa Catalina** ❶, in front of which an enormous, sail-like awning conceals a subterranean bus terminal. To the left, a shiny commercial centre, **El Muelle** (www.ccelmuelle.es), overlooks the port. Further north is the Poema del Mar (www.poema-del-mar.com; daily 9.30am–5.30pm), a modern aquarium that's breathed new life into this part of town.

PLAYA DE LAS CANTERAS

The stretch north from here along the huge **Puerto de la Luz** is all industrial buildings and traffic-clogged roads, so cross back to Parque Santa Catalina and make your way, via Calle Luís Morote, through the maze of streets to the beach.

Playa de las Canteras ❶ is the 3km (2-mile) stretch of sand that made the city Gran Canaria's very first tourist resort. It is lined with hotels and restaurants, some of which have been here since the 1960s heyday. A wide promenade runs the length of the beach; this busy walkway is dotted with palms, sun umbrellas that restaurants set out by the sea, and bright stalls piled high with clothing, carvings and jewellery.

Museo Elder is a fun science museum

These days, the beach is more popular with visiting mainland Spaniards than with northern Europeans and they use it to the full, forming circles to play bingo and setting up tables for huge picnic lunches. The top end of the beach has nets for volleyball and beach tennis, and the sea is often speckled with surfers. The natural reef, **La Barra**, a few hundred metres out, turns this stretch of coast into a natural lagoon, safe for children and non-swimmers.

LA ISLETA AND AROUND

At the northern tip of the beach, where the peninsula is at its narrowest, old wooden fishing boats are pulled up on the sand. Follow the road behind La Puntilla, a wind-tousled point jutting out to sea, to reach the old fishermen's quarter of **La Isleta** K. Here, you can visit the sombre Castillo de la Luz, now used as an exhibition centre (Tues–Sat 10am–7pm, Sun until 2pm) and the location of the **Fundación de Arte y Pensamiento Martín Chirino** (www.

fundacionmartinchirino.org), which showcases the sculptures of local artist Martín Chirino. The main reason to come here is to scale the highest peak at **Las Coloradas** for a sweeping view of the sea, the mountains and the city – and to eat in *El Padrino* (see page 106). It's a long, steep climb, though, and you would do better to take a taxi or a bus from Parque Santa Catalina.

At the southern end of Playa de las Canteras, beyond the reef's protective arm, constant onshore winds make ideal conditions for surfers. This once-neglected area has been smartened up, with a landscaped promenade leading to the **Auditorio Alfredo Kraus**, home to the Las Palmas Philharmonic Orchestra. A mammoth bronze statue of the tenor, who was born in the city, stands proudly outside. Seen from a distance, the sand-coloured building appears to rise from the sea, and in some lights blends into the hills behind. Across the road stands the huge **Las Arenas** commercial centre, which adjoins the stark Palacio de Congresos conference centre. From here, the arched bridge on the motorway heading northwest looks close enough to touch.

THE EAST

The lushest and loveliest corner of Gran Canaria is the eastern region. It takes in the verdant Barranco de Guayadeque, where a small community of people live in caves, and a string of towns with well-preserved historic centres. It also nudges into the area south of Arinaga, where strong winds power Pozo Izquierdo, Gran Canaria's biggest wind farm. Those same winds help competitors during the world championship windsurfing competitions held at Pozo Izquierdo. There are also surfing schools and other watersports available to tourists.

Driving down the GC-1 motorway from the airport or from Las Palmas, you will not be aware of the treasures that lie only a few kilometres inland. As faceless as most motorways, it is lined with factories, out-of-town megastores and an airforce base, all set in a bare, scrubby landscape. It is, of course, the fastest way to reach the areas of interest, but if you are not in a hurry, you could explore via minor roads.

> **Bus tips**
>
> If you visit the Jardín Canario by bus, ask the driver to tell you when you get there, or else he may not stop. Be prepared to cross the dual carriageway by an elevated pedestrian bridge to catch the bus back into town.

JARDÍN CANARIO

If you take the Santa Brígida road (GC-110) to the southwest of Las Palmas, you can include the **Jardín Canario Viera y Clavijo** ❷ (www.jardincanario.org; Mon–Fri

Discover local flora at Jardín Canario

7.30am–6pm, Sat–Sun 10am–6pm; free) on your itinerary. If you just want to make an excursion from Las Palmas to the garden, you can take bus No 303 (in the direction of San Mateo). They leave every fifteen minutes from the Parque San Telmo and the journey takes about twenty minutes. The botanical garden lies close to the suburb of Tafira Alta, where elegant, early twentieth-century villas and beautiful gardens are only slightly marred by the never-ending flow of traffic. The Jardín Canario is delightful, although the stepped, cobbled paths may rule it out for those who have difficulty getting around; some may wish that more of the fascinating specimens were identified.

The garden was established in 1952 by the Swedish botanist Eric R. Sventenius and is laid out along the steeply sloping side of a gorge. This can be crossed at one point by a wooden bridge to reach a flatter section where a cactus garden features an amazing selection of specimens from all over the world, many introduced to the island from the

Americas in the seventeenth century. Just past the main entrance, there are specimens of *Laurisilva* (bay laurel), which covered much of the island before the Spanish conquest but have long since been destroyed. There is also an avenue of dragon trees *(Dracaena draco),* which were once believed to have healing properties, and a grove of *Pinus canariensis,* the indigenous pine tree.

Allow a good couple of hours to visit the garden, because it is quite extensive and there is so much to see. Just outside the main entrance gate is a restaurant, which has a good reputation for serving typical Canarian food.

CALDERA DE BANDAMA

Just past Tafira Alta and Monte Lentiscal (the two prosperous suburbs virtually run into each other), drivers can take a left turn to the **Caldera de Bandama**. The volcanic crater is 1km (0.5 mile) wide and 200m (655ft) deep, and the best view of it is from the volcanic peak next door, the Pico de Bandama (574m/1,883ft), which has an observation platform and small bar – and you can drive to it. From here, you also take in magnificent views of the entire north and east coasts of the island. On a clear day, you can sometimes see the neighbouring island of Fuerteventura to the northeast, while to the west looms the central massif.

Adventurous visitors can climb down into the crater itself, via a steep path that is visible from the rim – it takes about thirty minutes. At the bottom is an abandoned farmhouse, shaded by two enormous eucalyptus trees, and the outlines of terraced fields where vines were once cultivated.

South of the caldera, which is the Spanish word for cauldron but has become the international geological term for a volcanic crater, lies the largest golf course on the island – and the oldest in Spain – the Real Club de Golf de Las Palmas. The club was founded at the end of the nineteenth century by some of the English expatriates

Colour-washed facades in Telde

who were so influential in the growth and prosperity of the city, and were eager to indulge in one of their favourite pastimes.

TELDE

Back on the main road, turn left at San José on the GC-80 to **Telde** ❸. Follow signs to San Juan or the Centro Histórico and park as soon as you can, because Telde, the second-largest town on the island, is bedevilled by narrow, one-way streets and far too much traffic. There is a large modern section that is of little interest to visitors, but the old town, a protected conservation area since 1981, is well worth a stop. It centres on the attractive Plaza de San Juan, shaded by mature trees and surrounded by colonial-style houses with beautiful mosaic tiles and intricately carved balconies. Lording it over the square is the **Iglesia de San Juan Bautista** (daily from 10.30am but only if a custodian is available). Building began in 1519, but the neo-Gothic towers are early twentieth-century additions. It houses a beautiful sixteenth-century Flemish altarpiece showing six scenes from the life of the Virgin, acquired when the town grew rich from the sugar trade. It is because the altarpiece is so valuable that the church is usually only open during services or when a guardian is available. The church's other treasure is an image of Christ made in Mexico from corn cobs. Just off the square is a children's park, with brightly coloured birds in an aviary.

The street that links San Juan with the other historic district, San Fernando, is named, like many others in Gran Canaria, after Fernando and Juan León y Castillo, the brothers who transformed the port of Las Palmas. They were born in Telde and their home is now the **Casa-Museo León y Castillo** (www.fernandoleonycastillo.com; Tues–Sun 10am–6pm). It contains Spanish paintings from the sixteenth to the twentieth centuries, along with sculpture and porcelain, and a library.

CUATRO PUERTAS

Telde was one of the two Guanche capitals before the Spanish arrived (Gáldar was the other) and the Indigenous people have left us an interesting archeological site, just off the GC-100 from Telde to Ingenio. **Cuatro Puertas** (always open; free), also known as Montaña Bermeja after the colour of its dark reddish stone, consists of a main chamber with four huge entrances. A shallow, semicircular enclave in the rock is thought to have been a sacrificial site, and the open space in front of the chamber was a tagoror, a place of assembly. The main cave is easily accessible, with excellent information boards explaining what you are looking at.

INGENIO

Around 5km (3 miles) along the GC-100 lies **Ingenio** ❹, an attractive little town famous for its delicacies such as *pan de puño* (fist bread), sold all over the island, and *sopa de la Virgen* (Virgin's soup). It was a prosperous sugar-refining centre in the sixteenth century (a model sugar press stands at the eastern approach to the town), but agriculture – chiefly tomato-growing – is the mainstay these days. Narrow alleys of whitewashed houses lead to the tiled **Plaza de la Candelaria**, where modern fountains contrast with a white, colonial-style church and the ochre-coloured town hall. Beside the church, bronze statues of women washing clothes add interest to another fountain. Between the church and town hall is the Tourist Office, which gives access to the Interpretation Centre of the Historical Heritage of Ingenio (tel: 928 783 799; call for opening times). This interactive space provides an illustrated journey back in time from the current history of the municipality to the pre-Hispanic era of the island.

BARRANCO DE GUAYADEQUE

Just before you reach the next town, Agüimes, 2km (1 mile) away, you will see a sign to the **Centro de Interpretación Arqueológica** (Tues–Sun 9am–5pm). This is the best route to take to the **Barranco de Guayadeque** ❺, well surfaced and less tortuous than the one from Ingenio, which also leads to the Interpretation Centre. The *barranco* is one of the most beautiful valleys on the island. Its steep slopes are honeycombed with cave dwellings (see box, page 46), and lush flora still thrives – cacti, tajinaste, palms and poppies, among other plantlife. The *barranco* is also home to one of the biggest lizards in the world – the *Lagarto canarión*; sparrow hawks can be seen in the skies and the sound of woodpeckers reverberates in the pine woods. There are still several functioning wells in the gorge; the Morro Verano, at 170m/555ft, is the deepest.

The *barranco* is for serious walkers, and there is a reliable organization in Agüimes that arranges hikes if you want to visit with a group (see page 89). If you go alone, make sure you have warm clothes for the chilly heights, strong shoes and plenty of water. However, there is much that can be enjoyed without doing anything too strenuous. The surfaced road continues for 9km (5

CAVE DWELLERS

The Centro de Interpretación is a helpful introduction to the life of the valley and its people, and displays some of the items – pottery, bones and textiles – that have been recovered from caves. More items are on display in the Museo Canario in Las Palmas. The *barranco* was the most densely populated gorge on the island during Guanche times. Early inhabitants farmed the slopes and even went down to the coast to fish, as the remains of sea-snail and limpet shells indicate. Numerous grain stores have been excavated and many mummified bodies were found in caves when interest in the area was stimulated at the end of the nineteenth century. The cave villages that exist today are rapidly being depleted. In 1970, there were some 450 inhabitants, now there are only about ninety. There are two chapels, and a functioning school, although it has fewer than a dozen pupils. Some crops are still grown – potatoes and corn in the higher regions, almonds on the lower slopes and on the valley floor – and some goats, pigs and sheep are kept, but most people now work in bars and restaurants, catering to the tourists.

miles) or so beyond the Interpretation Centre, passing glorious scenery and reaching two cave villages, both still viable communities, with tiny chapels, a bar and rudimentary restaurant, and houses bright with geraniums. The road ends at the best-known cave restaurant, the *Tagoror*.

AGÜIMES

Agüimes ❻ is one of the most appealing towns on the island. It's a place where the Ayuntamiento (Town Hall) takes seriously the job of preserving and improving the environment, and fostering conservation-conscious tourism – and it shows. The outskirts of the town, where there is a bus station and a public swimming pool, is pleasant enough, but the **Casco Histórico** is the place to go.

Spotless, narrow streets of ochre- and terracotta-coloured houses – several of them converted into *casa rural* accommodation – lead to the shady main square, **Plaza de Nuestra Señora del Rosario**, flanked by bars and cafés. Here, and in other parts of town, a smattering of bronze statues has been erected, portraying rural life and local characters. The Neoclassical **Iglesia de San Sebastián** (daylight hours) at one end of the square, is a designated Monumento Histórico Artístico and has works by island sculptor José Luján Pérez. The Museo de Historia de Agüimes (Tues–Sun 9am–2pm & 3–6pm) at Calle Juan Alvarado y Saz 42 is also worth a visit if you're interested in local history. The tourist office, on Plaza San Antón, has an information centre filled with old photos and historical pieces.

Soft classical music spills out from hidden speakers around a bronze statue of a female cellist.

ARINAGA

For a real contrast, make the short trip from Agüimes to sleepy little **Arinaga**. As you will soon realize, this is a windy stretch of coast – one much in favour with windsurfers. There is also a marine reserve and diving centre, at **Playa del Cabrón**. What is most immediately obvious, south of Arinaga, are the huge, graceful and surprisingly quiet wind turbines producing energy at the Pozo Izquierdo plant. Pozo Izquierdo beach is the site of events in the PWA World Cup Championships.

THE SOUTHERN RESORTS

The southern resorts of Gran Canaria are synonymous with package holidays, where sun, sea and sand keep visitors happy by day, and bars and clubs ensure the alcohol is flowing and the music thumping until the early hours of the morning. The resorts of San Agustín, Playa del Inglés and Maspalomas, mini-cities built to provide instant gratification, were created out of this desert-by-the-sea and therefore have no history; no corners where remnants of an earlier way of life linger on. What they do have is year-round good weather, miles of rolling sands, watersports facilities, hotels and apartments with lush gardens and landscaped swimming pools; and restaurants, clubs, bars and shops by the score.

To the west of the three main resorts lie Puerto Rico and Puerto de Mogán. The former is also an artificial creation, but smaller and more low-key than its neighbours, and with an emphasis on family entertainment and watersports of all kinds. The latter was a struggling little fishing village until the tourist boom and has since been transformed into a delightful little resort built around a series of canals, with a wonderful sheltered harbour for yachtsmen.

SAN AGUSTÍN

Whether you are coming direct from the airport, from Las Palmas, or from Agüimes, you will approach the resorts on the GC-1 motorway. The first one, **San Agustín** ❼, was also the first to be built, in 1962. There is a plethora of hotels and apartment blocks, some cut off from the beach by the main road, over which there is a pedestrian bridge. The resort is growing, but it is still the smallest and quietest of the big three and caters mainly for retired couples and families with young children, although it is also very popular with windsurfers (the BD Windsurf Centre is here). There is a fairly small, safe beach, a variety of watersports kiosks and some attractive apartments, most set in gardens among palms and poinsettia, and with their own pools.

Following the paved promenade to the west of the resort, you reach **Playa de las Burras**, known as Playa Chica – the little beach – around which cluster a villa complex, a well-stocked supermarket, a small shopping centre and a string of modern apartment blocks and hotels.

PLAYA DEL INGLÉS

You can walk along the beachfront promenade from San Agustín to **Playa del Inglés** ❽. As you stroll, you will notice that the sand becomes more golden, the apartment blocks grow taller and bars louder. Approach from the motorway and you will find yourself suddenly in a grid of wide streets lined with large hotels, restaurants, car-hire outlets and a huddle of shops, and peopled by a relentless march of tourists carrying beach gear.

Playa del Inglés is a big place, but there is a good bus service and a supply of cheap and reliable taxis; hotels further from the beach usually provide frequent free buses. There are several huge commercial centres, the largest being the **Yumbo Centre**, which is in need of a facelift but still seems to attract a large crowd in the evening. Among the cluster of bars and clubs in the centre are quite a few venues that cater to the LGBTQ+ community.

The beach is the main event, of course. The **Paseo Costa Canaria** is an attractive pedestrian promenade, lined with villa complexes and bright with tropical blooms. The walkway runs the length of the sandy swathe, from Playa de las Burras all the way to the Maspalomas dunes. On the bleached sands below, sun loungers and beach umbrellas are arranged in serried ranks, and out at sea the more energetic visitors try their hand at water-skiing, windsurfing and parasailing.

Descend via stairs or escalators to the **Paseo Marítimo**. Protected by awnings from the heat of the sun, this is a 2km

(1.25-mile) stretch of fast-food haunts, amusement arcades, Irish pubs and German beer kellers with extended happy hours, tattoo parlours, internet cafés and shops selling beachwear.

MASPALOMAS

Maspalomas is divided from Playa del Inglés by a spectacular stretch of **dunes**, sprawling across an area of 4 sq km (1.5 sq miles), that in 1994 were designated a nature reserve in order to preserve the ecosystem. The contrast between these pristine mountains of sand and the commercialism of the resort is quite remarkable. You can walk over the dunes if you protect your feet from the hot sand, but it is hard-going and takes over an hour. Following the beach around takes half the time, and you will pass a popular nudist stretch en route. Adjoining the dunes, a golf course forms another

Playa del Inglés, a tourist hotspot

barrier between the neighbourhoods, but inland the two resorts almost merge into each other, although their style is distinctive. Accommodation in Maspalomas is in smart hotels, bungalows or low-rise apartment complexes set in large, lush gardens, for this is altogether a more upmarket resort.

The main road swoops past **Aqualand** waterpark (daily 10am–5pm; www.aqualand.es) and the huge **Holiday World** amusement park (www.holidayworld-maspalomas.com; daily 4–11pm), all the way round the sprawling Maspalomas development to **El Faro**, the lighthouse. From here, a palm-lined *paseo* leads to the area known as **El Oasis**, with some smart hotels and other more affordable

THE COUNT'S VISION

The Conde del Castillo de la Vega Grande de Guadelupe, an aristocrat with a pedigree as long as his name, had a family home in Telde, in a building that is now the town hall. He also had large tracts of unused and seemingly useless land in the barren south of the island. Nobody lived there, nothing would grow there and the land was a liability. In the early 1960s, however, as the tourist boom swept through mainland Spain, the count came up with a scheme that would change the face and the economy of Gran Canaria. Out of the desert, he constructed what are now the resorts of San Agustín, Playa del Inglés and Maspalomas. Tour companies, quick to spot a potential gold mine, soon moved building contractors in. Where else would you find streets named after tour operators as you do in Maspalomas? Within two decades, the south of Gran Canaria had mushroomed into a huge holiday complex, attracting visitors from northern Europe, mainly on all-inclusive package holidays, providing employment for islanders and further enriching the man who masterminded the project.

The undulating dunes of Maspalomas

apartments, beside **La Charca** (see box, page 54). You can drive back up Avenida Oceania, which parallels a palm-fringed dry riverbed that runs straight through the middle of the *urbanización*.

To the west of the lighthouse, in a sheltered bay, lies the quieter resort of Meloneras, with more luxury hotels and bungalow accommodation. Further inland, **Sonnenland** is a low-key, family-oriented tourist complex.

INLAND EXCURSIONS

When the swimming pool loses its sparkle and the beach becomes a bore, there are plenty of excursions available inland. A car isn't necessary because there are regular bus services from convenient stops in all the resorts. **Mundo Aborigen** (daily 9am–6pm), a well-structured recreation of life in a Guanche settlement, and the **Camel Safari Park La Baranda** (www.camelsafarigrancanaria.com; Mon–Sat 9am–5pm) are both a few kilometres up the road to

Fataga, while **Palmitos Park** (www.palmitospark.es; daily 10am–6pm), a vast ornithological park with an aquarium, butterfly house and botanic garden, is on the road inland from Maspalomas. **Sioux City** (www.parquetematicosiouxcitypark.com; Tues–Sun 10am–4pm), a Wild West theme park, lies in the Cañon del Águila, just east of San Agustín.

PUERTO RICO

The GC-1 motorway continues along the coast to Puerto Rico. The first community west of Maspalomas (on the old coast road) is **Pasito Blanco**, a little port and resort mainly of interest to sailing enthusiasts. Next comes **Arguineguín**, which has witnessed a surge of development in recent years but is still a working fishing port and community and rather pleasant after so much artificiality. Elderly men playing draughts in the Centro Socio Cultural seem unaffected by the comings and goings of the tourists who disembark from pleasure craft, mostly bound for the larger resorts nearby. For developers looking to expand a pleasant little bay surrounded by sheer cliffs, it is easy enough to build a landscaped promenade and a few attractive seaside villas, but after that the only way is up.

That is what the entrepreneurs of **Puerto Rico** ❿ did when the resort was greenlit in the 1970s. The result: a wall of apartment blocks rising to the top of the hills, like tiers of seats in a giant amphitheatre. Below, space is at a premium, and sunbeds are even lined up along the length of the

> ### La Charca
>
> La Charca, part of the Maspalomas nature reserve, is a little lagoon to which migratory and breeding birds, frightened away by human activity, are being encouraged to return. Moorhens, herons and kestrels have ventured back to its reed beds and ospreys have occasionally been seen.

jetty. The clean little beach is family-oriented and children will love the **Angry Birds Activity Park** (www.activityparkcanarias.com; Thurs–Mon 10am–6pm). There are also several large, modern commercial centres.

Puerto Rico has a serious reputation as a sailing centre, and members of its club have won several Olympic medals. Deep-sea fishermen, not to be outdone, have claimed around three-dozen world records in their sport. Naturally, the **Puerto Deportivo** caters for visiting fishing and watersports enthusiasts. There are diving centres and sailing schools, deep-sea fishing trips, dolphin-spotting trips in glass-bottomed catamarans, or simple pleasure trips that wend along the scenic coastline.

Playa de Amadores, a sandy arc near Puerto Rico

PUERTO DE MOGÁN

Built round a complex of seawater canals with delicately arched bridges, **Puerto de Mogán** ⓫ is almost impossibly pretty. The windows and flat roofs of its two-storey houses are outlined in shades of blue, green and ochre, the walls smothered with multicoloured bougainvillaea and trailing geraniums.

There are two ports here: the working one that was once the town's *raison d'être* and from which a fishing fleet still operates, and the **Puerto Deportivo**, where luxurious yachts bob in the water. This leisure port is lined with cafés and restaurants, all offering

Puerto Rico's amphitheatre of apartment blocks

wonderful views and boat-fresh fish and seafood menus. The string of buildings in the narrow streets behind the harbour is equally picturesque; some have been reimagined as restaurants and gift shops, but most are holiday apartments belonging to the *Hotel Puerto de Mogán* (see page 137).

Submarine Adventure offers trips in a yellow submarine, and pleasure boats ply back and forth between here, Puerto Rico and Arguineguín. However, most visitors are content simply to wander the sun-drenched streets and sit in the pavement cafés, or make for the small, sheltered beach to the east of the port, which has been 'sandscaped' and extended.

On Friday, a huge market spills along the quay, selling African carvings, bead jewellery, aromatherapy oils, island cheeses, fresh fruits, and beach sarongs. Busloads of tourists arrive from neighbouring resorts around 10.30am and are whisked away with their purchases in the afternoon.

MOGÁN

The road inland climbs up the fertile, fruit-producing *barranco* to Mogán. In season, you may be able to buy ripe papaya, mangoes and avocados from streetside stalls. Just before the town, a windmill stands sentinel by the road in the tiny hamlet of El Molino de Viento – which means windmill. Surrounded by jagged mountains, **Mogán** ⑫ is a sleepy little place with a picture-postcard church dedicated to San Antonio; colourful, well-watered gardens in the central plaza; and towering palms outside the town hall. If you come in high season, when visitors drive up from the coast in hired jeeps, there will be a buzz of activity on the streets and in a couple of rather good restaurants. Otherwise, the sound of goats bleating in the *barranco* may be the only noise you hear during your stay.

GOING WEST

The west of Gran Canaria is for those who like a challenge. It is the area least visited by tourists; the roads are vertiginous and villages few and far between. But there are stunning rock formations and mountain landscapes, marvellous views and a chance to experience a region that feels quite remote, although it's only a few hours' drive from Las Palmas.

THE MOUNTAIN ROUTE

The road from Mogán (GC-200) twists and turns on its way to San Nicolás de Tolentino, cutting through rocks of red, grey and gold

Fishing fiestas

The Fiestas del Carmen, celebrating the patron saint of fishermen, take place throughout July in Arguineguín and Puerto de Mogán. Celebrations include firework displays, concerts and dances, and culminate in a maritime procession, led by a decorated boat carrying the statue of the Virgin.

and passing isolated houses where convolvulus clings to crumbling walls. To your right soar the Montaña de Sándara, the Montaña de las Monjas, and the peak of Inagua, all nudging above 1400m (4600ft) high. To the left, three deep gorges run down to the sea. The first is the **Barranco de Veneguera**, where a track – which should only be attempted in a 4WD vehicle – leads 10km (6 miles) through banana plantations to a lovely, unspoiled beach. The *barranco* is part of the Parque Rural del Nublo and cannot be developed for tourism.

The road wending through the next gorge, the **Barranco de Tasarte**, is in better condition, and also culminates in a pretty beach. From the third gully, the **Barranco de Tasártico**, there is a long, arduous hike through the **Reserva Natural Especial de Güi-Güi**, where 3000 hectares (7400 acres) of land are protected to safeguard the vegetation clinging to the rocks. Those who go

The fishing fleet at Puerto de Mogán

the distance will be rewarded with an idyllic little beach. Just past the Tasarte turning, to the right of the road, is **La Fuente de los Azulejos**, where oxidization has turned the rocks bright green. Opposite, a roadside bar sells papaya juice to refresh weary drivers and aloe vera to ease sunburnt hikers.

SAN NICOLÁS DE TOLENTINO

As the road begins to straighten, you come to the village of **Tocodomán**. Here, you will find **Cactualdea** (www.cactualdea.es; daily 10.30am–5pm). This 'cactus village' is home to more members of the spiky plant family than you knew existed, all well labelled and set among palms and dragon trees. There is also a replica Guanche cave, a restaurant serving typical Canarian dishes, wine-tasting opportunities and, of course, a handy gift shop.

You won't be able to miss the fact that swathes of land here are covered in plastic. Beneath the sheets grow tomatoes, the crop that is the mainstay of the region and of its only proper town, **San Nicolás de Tolentino** (officially known as La Aldea de San Nicolás). The town does not have a lot going for it, but it's a friendly place that tries hard to attract visitors. A tourist office on the right as you enter town offers informative leaflets and has *artesanía* items for sale, the woven textiles showing distinct Latin American influences. The town used to be a craft centre but these days weaving and pottery are hobbies rather than industries. Otherwise, there is a smattering of small hotels and a couple of restaurants offering 'home-style cooking'.

PUERTO DE LA ALDEA

Some 3km (2 miles) down the road is **Puerto de la Aldea** ⓭ – which simply means 'port of the village'. The harbour is tiny, but there seems to be enough fish brought in to keep a few restaurants flourishing. Beside a pebbly beach is a smartly tiled promenade;

THE COASTAL ROAD

parallel to it runs a shady garden scattered with stone picnic tables set beneath pine trees. At the far end lies **El Charco** (The Lagoon), a fairly nondescript pond for most of the year but on 11 September the site of the Fiesta del Charco, when local people attempt to catch fish with their bare hands and to duck each other in the water. The origins of this curious custom are uncertain, but it is believed to date from pre-Hispanic times. *Lucha canaria* (wrestling) matches and *juego del palo* (stick-fighting) competitions are an integral part of the festival.

An Indigenous settlement close by, **Los Caserones**, has yielded a great many archeological finds, including the bones of a Verdino dog, the emblem of the Canary Islands. The crumbling remains can be seen on a small hill.

THE COASTAL ROAD

The journey along the coast demands concentration. The road wends between bare rock on one side and steep cliffs, plunging straight into the ocean, on the other. Fortunately, two *miradores* (viewpoints) have been created at points of particular beauty, so drivers can safely stop to admire the views. The first is the **Mirador del Balcón**, the second the **Andén Verde**. To the north, the craggy coastline runs up to the Punto de Góngora; straight ahead, across miles of dark blue sea, lies Tenerife, crowned with the peak of El Teide, at 3718m (11,898ft)

You say tomato

The tomato industry is not as prosperous as it once was, as it now faces stiff competition from Moroccan growers. Despite this, the region still exports some 100,000kg (220,000lbs) of early varieties a year. The *tomate aliñado* is a popular tapas dish: a huge local tomato comes sliced, drizzled in olive oil and vinegar, and topped off with lashings of garlic.

The view from the Mirador del Balcón

the highest mountain in Spain. The road here is prone to rock falls and is occasionally inaccessible. The first phase of a new motorway between El Risco and Andén Verde, which darts through a 3km tunnel, provides an alternative route.

PUERTO DE LAS NIEVES

There are still many curves to navigate before you arrive at **Puerto de las Nieves** (The Harbour of the Snows). The name derives not from any freak snowfall but from Nuestra Señora de las Nieves, the Madonna of the Snows, patron saint of the local fishermen. Her tiny chapel, known as the **Ermita de las Nieves** (by appointment only outside Mass times), houses a real treasure, a sixteenth-century Flemish triptych attributed to Joos van Cleve, depicting the Virgin and Child flanked by saints Francis and Anthony. The decorated wooden ceiling above the choir is said to be Mudéjar, the architecture of the Moors who remained in Spain after the reconquest in the late eleventh century.

In the harbour, fishing boats bob gently beside a jetty, where wooden decking has been laid down for the benefit of sunbathers who can't find a comfortable spot on the pebble beach. There is a sheltered bay, which is good for swimming. A cluster of restaurants lines the quay, serving excellent fish at reasonable prices. They get very busy at weekends, when people from Las Palmas come for lunch. Otherwise, the main bursts of activity are the arrivals and departures of the ferries to Santa Cruz de Tenerife, run by the Fred Olsen line (a free bus from Las Palmas connects with the port).

A great deal of investment has gone into the village in an attempt to compensate for the declining fishing industry. A large hotel has been built close to the remains of a Guanche cemetery, but on the whole the development has been sympathetic. A promenade, called the Paseo de los Poetas, has been constructed, and some low-rise apartment blocks and villas have sprung up in the streets behind it, blending well with the single-storey fishermen's cottages.

BRINGING DOWN THE BRANCHES

Puerto de las Nieves and Agaete are renowned for a festival known as Bajada de las Ramas (Bringing Down the Branches), celebrated with great enthusiasm on 4–5 August each year. Residents of the two communities gather branches from the hillsides and carry them down to the harbour, where they whip the waves with them before laying them at the feet of the Virgin of the Snows. Although this provides a religious context, the ritual has pagan origins, and, like many festivals, was intended to bring both rain and fertility. It's a high-spirited occasion, with lots of music and dancing, feasting and frolicking, and people come from all over the island to take part.

At the southern end of the village, the stump of the **Dedo de Dios** (Finger of God) rises from the sea. The 'finger' itself, once a famous local landmark, was destroyed by a storm in 2005.

AGAETE

Return to the main road and almost immediately you are in **Agaete** ⓯, where a number of the houses are punctuated with carved wooden balconies. In the Plaza de la Constitución, as you enter the town, stands the imposing, nineteenth-century Iglesia de la Concepción. Nearby, off Calle Huertas, the **Huerto de las Flores** (Tues–Sat 10am–4pm; free) is a small botanical garden planted with a selection of rare trees and colourful plants.

On the outskirts is the **Parque Arqueológico de Maipés** (www.arqueologiacanaria.com; Tues–Sun 10am–5pm in winter, until

Celebrating the patron saint of fishermen, Puerto de las Nieves

The dramatic Barranco de Agaete

6pm in summer), a Guanche necropolis. The town stands at the head of the **Barranco de Agaete**, a fertile, emerald-green gorge signposted **El Valle** (The Valley). It's a lovely place to drive or walk. Avocados, oranges, lemons and mangoes grow on terraces, clinging to the valley walls. Tall Canary palms, solitary agaves and prickly pears gradually give way, on the upper slopes, to the Canary pine. The road only tracks as far as the little village of Los Berrazales. Just before you reach it, a dirt track diverts to the atmospheric *Finca Las Longueras* (www.laslongueras.com), a *hotel rural* housed in a nineteenth-century colonial mansion (see page 138).

THE NORTH

There are some 700 hectares (1730 acres) of protected land in the north of the island; the best known is the **Reserva Natural de los Tilos de Moya**. Away from these reserves, the terrain is fairly barren, for the forests of bay laurel (*Laurus canariensis*) that once coloured the landscape green were cut down in the sixteenth century to provide fuel for the sugar industry. Yet more land was cleared to make way for bananas, introduced as a monocrop by the English more than three centuries later. The principal crop today is still bananas, many of which are grown in mammoth plastic tunnels.

In marked contrast to the sparsely populated west coast, this small area encompasses half a dozen towns: Gáldar, Guía, Moya, Arucas, Firgas and Teror. All are worth visiting and all involve circuitous, winding roads. It is often easier to return to the main coastal road between towns, rather than take what looks like the shortest route.

GÁLDAR

The hill on which **Gáldar** ⓰ is set resembles an extinct volcano, with the town clustered at its feet. It is only about 8km (5 miles) between Agaete and Gáldar, but the pace of life seems to shift up a few gears. Park as soon as you find a space because traffic is heavy, and the one-way streets are confusing.

Gáldar is known as the Ciudad de los Guanartemes (City of Rulers), as it was the seat of Tenesor Semidan, one of the island's two Guanche Chiefs. The town is proud of its heritage and many of the streets and squares have Guanche names. Post-conquest

Gáldar was founded in 1484 and was the capital of Gran Canaria before Las Palmas.

The **Iglesia de Santiago de los Caballeros**, in a shady square, was built on the spot where Semidan's palace supposedly stood. Begun in 1778, it was the first Neoclassical building on the island. It houses a number of statues attributed to José Luján Pérez (1756–1815), who was born nearby in Santa María de Guía. The Ayuntamiento (Town Hall), in the same square, has a huge dragon tree in its courtyard. Planted in 1718, it is said to be the oldest in the archipelago. At the side of the square, you will find the tourist office and the Teatro Municipal.

The Patrimonio Histórico – the department in charge of cultural affairs – was somewhat slow to exploit Galdár's legacy, but the Museo y Parque Arqueológico Cueva Pintada (www.cuevapintada.com; Tues–Sat 10am–6pm, Sun 11am–6pm) is now open in Calle Audiencia, in the town centre, on the site of the Guanche Painted Cave. Visitors can buy tickets in advance on site and through the website. Another important archeological site, reached by a lane running through banana plantations towards the coast, is the **Poblado y Necrópolis de la Guancha**, consisting of the remains of circular tombs and a cluster of houses, where numerous mummies were found.

SARDINA

From the roundabout to the west of Gáldar (the same way you came in), the main road west leads to **Sardina**, a tiny resort hugging a small beach, popular with snorkellers and protected by dark,

Guanche sculptures

At the eastern entrance to Gáldar, a sculpture represents three Guanche princesses. Another sculpture in the town depicts Tenesor Semidan, the Chief who was forced to accept baptism and collaborate with the Spanish.

volcanic rocks. A harbourside restaurant offers excellent fish dishes and a view of the beach. Sardina is quiet during the week but attracts people from Gáldar and Las Palmas at weekends. North of the village, a lighthouse stands on the windy Punta de Sardina.

SANTA MARÍA DE GUÍA

The next town, going east from Gáldar at the same roundabout, is little **Santa María de Guía** ⑰, usually just known as Guía, famous for its award-winning *queso de flor*. This is a cheese made from sheep and cow milk, mixed with the juice of cardoon thistle flowers. A traditional cheese festival is held here at the end of April and beginning of May and continues in nearby Montaña Alta.

There are some attractive, brightly painted houses in Guía's Casco Histórico, and an imposing, two-towered church in the Plaza Grande (not as huge as its name might suggest) where a market is held every Tuesday morning.

CENOBIO DE VALERÓN

Take the main road now for Moya, but turn off first where you see signs to the **Cenobio de Valerón** ⑱ (www.arqueologiacanaria.com; Tues–Sun winter 10am–5pm, summer 10am–6pm). *Cenobio* means convent and this complex of some 300 caves, hollowed out of the soft, volcanic rock, was once believed to have been a place where *harimagüadas* – young virgins – were detained in order to protect their purity until they married. However, it is now widely accepted that the caves were grain stores, which were easily defensible because of their isolated position.

MOYA

The GC-75 – the next turning off the main road – winds uphill to friendly, sleepy little **Moya** ⑲. There is a helpful tourist office and an impressive church, **Nuestra Señora de Candelaria**, begun in

The pre-Hispanic Cenobio de Valerón

the sixteenth century but with many later additions. It is home to some interesting pieces of sculpture, including a fifteenth-century cedarwood figure of the Virgin of Candelaria, and several works by Luján Pérez, but unfortunately it is often closed except for early evening services.

Moya is the birthplace of the island's best-loved poet, Tomás Morales (1885–1921) and his home, the **Casa-Museo Morales** (www.tomasmorales.com; Tues–Sun 10am–6pm), stands in the square opposite the church. It's an intimate little place with first editions of Morales' work, his Remington typewriter and lots of photos, paintings and poems. A bronze statue of the poet stands outside. Morales is one of the poets after whom the Paseo de los Poetas in Puerto de las Nieves was named. The other two are his contemporaries, Alonso Quesada and Saulo Torón.

From the top of the town, a road leads past neatly cultivated vegetable gardens on the valley slopes to **Los Tilos de Moya**, a

91-hectare (225-acre) nature reserve – although it is laurels, not *tilos* (limes), that are protected here. Swathes of them once cloaked the island but few remain, and the protection order has been placed in an attempt to re-establish them.

ARUCAS

Unless you want to visit the centre of the island, retrace your route to the main coast road or motorway and at Bañaderos, take the turning to **Arucas** ⓴. As you enter the town, the **Parque Municipal** is on your left, a shady spot full of exotic trees and plants. You will soon get pulled into the busy one-way system, so park as soon as possible and explore the **Casco Histórico** on foot. The huge lava-stone church of **San Juan Bautista** (daily 9.30am–12.30pm, 4.30–7pm; free), begun in 1909, is said to owe its inspiration to Antoni Gaudí's Sagrada Família in Barcelona, and there are some similar Modernista flourishes. Inside, it is more conventionally neo-Gothic, and has three splendid rose windows.

In the nearby Calle León y Castillo, a statue of the poet Domingo Rivero, book in hand, stands in front of a giant cactus outside the Casa de Cultura. Rivero, great-uncle of Tomás Morales, was born here in 1852. Inside, leading off a pleasant courtyard with a dragon tree, are much-frequented reading rooms for adults and children.

One of the reasons traffic is heavy in Arucas is that tourists' vehicles must wend their way through the old town to reach the nearby **Montaña de Arucas**. This is where the Guanche leader, Doramas, was killed in single-handed combat by Pedro de Vera in 1480. His followers are said to have leapt to their deaths in the *barranco* rather than surrender. Today, there's an observation point overlooking the countryside.

FIRGAS AND THE FINCA DE OSORIO

From Arucas, there are two routes to Teror. The longer one, on the GC-300, will take you via the pleasant little town of **Firgas**, where a man-made waterfall cascades 30m (90ft) down shallow steps in the centre of a pedestrianized street.

Firgas is known for its water. There's a natural spring just south of the town and the remarkably tasty product is bottled and sold all over the island.

A lava-stone church dominates Arucas

The more direct route is on the GC-43. This one will take you past the **Finca de Osorio** (not open to the public). This rural mansion is used as an *Aula de la Naturaleza* – a place where school groups and college students come, some on residential courses, to learn about conservation, wildlife and agriculture.

TEROR

Teror ㉑ is a delightful little town with some of the best examples of colonial-style architecture you will find outside Las Palmas. Carved wooden balconies adorn sugar-white facades and huge doors open onto fern-filled courtyards. It is also the home of Virgen del Pino (Madonna of the Pine Tree). In 1481, as the island was being subdued by the forces of Pedro de Vera, local shepherds are said to have had a vision of the Virgin appearing to them at the top of a pine tree. The miraculous apparition gave rise to a cult, and today the town has a clutch of lovely churches dedicated to the Virgin. In the centre stands the **Basilica de Nuestra Señora del Pino** (Mon–Fri 11am–3pm, Sat–Sun 11am–2.30pm; free), begun in 1767, where the richly clothed statue of the Virgin is displayed, surrounded by votive gifts and symbols. The Virgin del Pino is perhaps the best-loved saint on the island and pilgrims flock to Teror all year round, but especially on her feast day, 8 September. A huge festival is held during that week, with traditional music and dancing and plenty of cheerful secular celebrations accompanying sombre religious rituals.

Behind the church are stalls selling local produce – home-made bread, cheese and vegetables – as well as

> ### Virgin's gifts
>
> A sensible sign in the Basilica de Nuestra Señora del Pino poignantly reads: 'Although the Virgin is grateful for your gifts and candles she would rather you gave your money to the poor.'

religious items. In front stands the Palacio Episcopal (Bishop's Palace), which now houses a cultural centre. On the right-hand side of the basilica is the **Casa Museo de los Patronos de la Virgen del Pino** (tel: 928 630 239; Sun–Fri 11am–6pm) in a beautiful building, set around a courtyard and furnished in the style of a noble, seventeenth-century home. It belongs, as it always has, to the Manrique de Lara family, who still spend the festival week here. At the back of the house are an old bakery and a stable block, where Don Manrique's polished 1951 Triumph shares space with sedan chairs, carts and carriages.

There is a smaller square close by, the **Plaza Teresa de Bolívar**, with a stone fountain in the centre. It is named after the first wife of Simón de Bolívar, the man who led the liberation of many of the Spanish colonies in South America in the nineteenth century. Her family came from Teror; his from Tenerife. The couple met in Venezuela, but Teresa died less than a year after they were married.

The centre of Teror is closed to traffic, so you can wander through the cobbled alleys and little squares and drink in the atmosphere without being disturbed by noise or fumes. If you come on Sunday morning you will also be able to enjoy the busy, and very local, market.

THE CENTRAL PEAKS

In order to appreciate the age and majesty of the planet and the relative insignificance of human beings, all you need is a trip to the central peaks of Gran Canaria. Over millions of years, the rocky landscape has been moulded into strange shapes by volcanic eruptions, fierce winds and driving rain, and erosion has also scored deep *barrancos* (gorges) that plunge to the coast, their fertile soil supporting lush vegetation.

The highest summits are Pico de las Nieves (Peak of the Snows) at 1949m (6394ft), followed by Roque Nublo (Rock of Clouds), at 1803m (5915ft), and Roque Bentaiga (1412m/4632ft). Beneath them, mountain villages cling to the sheer rock, and narrow terraces are cultivated wherever possible. Much of the central area is protected as part of the Parque Rural del Nublo; while the land to the west of Artenara forms the Parque Natural de Tamadaba. While the mountains lure climbers and serious walkers to their challenging contours, there are many relatively short and easy walks that can be made amid stunning scenery, some of them on the *caminos reales* (see page 80), others on newer paths.

The central region can be reached easily from most parts of the island: direct from Las Palmas; from the northern towns of Arucas and Moya; from Agüimes in the east; or from the southern resorts, via the Barranco de Fataga. It is only from the wild west coast, where tracks either peter out altogether or challenge the toughest vehicles and most confident drivers, that the peaks prove inaccessible.

VEGA DE SAN MATEO | 75

If you're approaching from Las Palmas, you can take the Santa Brígida road through **Vega de San Mateo** (usually known simply as San Mateo) and up the tortuous road to Tejeda, where bus drivers sound their horns in warning as they approach every sharp bend. Or you could avoid the stress and take bus No. 303, changing in Vega de San Mateo. This colourful little town has a large food and craft market on Sunday and charming shops full of farm-to-fork food and artisanal products. As the road climbs upwards, the lush vegetation changes. If you visit in spring or early summer, you will notice rampaging nasturtiums, blossoming lavender bushes and neat orange groves on the first part of the journey. Next come the prickly pear cactus *(Opuntia ficus indica)*, eucalyptus trees and century plants *(Agave)*, before the entire hillside turns yellow with broom and, close to the top, the pines and holm oaks begin.

CRUZ DE TEJEDA

The top of the pass, at 1580m (5184ft), is marked by a sombre, stone crucifix, the **Cruz de Tejeda** ㉒. Surrounded by towering peaks, this is a hive of commercial activity, with bustling restaurants (one, *El Refugio*, is also a hotel; www.hotelruralelrefugio.com), a shop selling local food specialities, and a row of stalls piled with everything from embroidered tablecloths to dried fruit and stuffed camels.

Behind the cross stands a hotel, the beautifully renovated four-star **Parador Hotel de Cruz de Tejeda** (see page 139), designed in the 1930s by Néstor Martín-Fernández de la Torre. Magnificent panoramic views can be enjoyed from the hotel, as well as a spa and fitness facilities.

The view is dominated by the impressive, pointing finger of **Roque Nublo** ㉓, which will have been visible for some time. Depending on the weather and the time of day, the volcanic monolith appears to change colour and it is not hard to understand why the Guanches revered this vast rock formation as a holy place. *A camino reale* leads from Cruz de Tejeda to Roque Nublo, but there is a shorter walk from Ayacata. On a clear day, especially, there is a breathtaking view across the island. Away in the distance, Tenerife's Mt Teide, snow-capped for much of the year, seems to rise straight out of the sea.

ARTENARA

It is a challenging but beautiful drive from Tejeda to **Artenara** ㉔, which, at an altitude of 1270m (4167ft), is the highest village on the island. It also one of the oldest, pre-dating the Spanish conquest, and Artenara is its Guanche name. Many of the houses in the village are built into the solid rock, although some of them, with their painted facades, look like ordinary houses, and most have modern amenities. The cave church, **La Ermita de la Cuevita**, is only identified by a bell above the door. It houses the *Virgen de la Cuevita*, whose festival is celebrated at the end of August. The Iglesia de San Matías is a more conventional church.

Mirador La Cilla (see page 112) is on most visitors' itineraries, a cave restaurant entered via a long tunnel. It has a sunny terrace with fine views of Roque Bentaiga and Roque Nublo, and the hearty island dishes – including *ropa vieja* (beef and tomato stew), *papas arrugadas* (wrinkled potatoes) and grilled meats – are good value.

PINAR DE TAMADABA

From Artenara, a road leads around the **Pinar de Tamadaba** ㉕, 8 sq km (3 sq miles) of protected forest within a much larger nature park, where Canary pines *(Pinus canariensis)* grow to enormous heights, untroubled by pollution – some reach almost 60m (190ft). Forest fires occur periodically, but the pine is capable of rapid regeneration. There are footpaths through the forest, but great care must be taken not to cause fires or in any way damage the environment. The road does not lead beyond the *pinar*, so you have to return the way you came.

BARRANCO DE FATAGA

If you are approaching the central peaks from the south, take the Fataga road from Playa del Inglés. This leads through the beautiful **Barranco de Fataga**, where burnished walls of rock are reminiscent of canyons in the American West. After an easy start, the bends in the road become tighter and the valley is greener. Palm trees line the roadside and tropical fruits are cultivated on the valley floor.

Passing the popular Mundo Aborigen and the Camel Safari Park, you soon arrive in the village of **Fataga**, perched precipitously on a rock jutting out into the gorge. There is a nice church and several cheerful restaurants, some of them offering barbecues and live music, catering to visitors on jeep safaris from the coast.

The road winds towards **San Bartolomé de Tirajana** ㉖, a historic little town, the administrative centre of a region that includes Maspalomas and Playa del Inglés. The town's main source of income is the production of fruit, especially cherries. The Ayuntamiento (Town Hall) has an attractive inner courtyard, and there are two churches – the Neoclassical San Bartolomé, outside which a market is held on Sunday morning, and Santiago el Apóstol. The festival of Santiago (St James) is a major event on 25 July. You may want to stop at the petrol station here for petrol, as garages are few and far between in the mountains.

> **Mountain liqueurs**
>
> The mountain regions specialize in liqueurs. *Guindilla* is a punchy cherry liqueur made in San Bartolomé, which takes its name from the Spanish word for morello cherries – *guindas*. *Mejunje* is a sweet concoction of rum, honey and lemon that was traditionally served to priests when they visited their parishioners at home.

PICO DE LAS NIEVES AND ROQUE BENTAIGA

Following signs to Tejeda, you will reach the little village of **Ayacata**, from where there is a popular and fairly undemanding walk to Roque Nublo, which takes about forty minutes each way. It passes another, smaller rock figure known as El Fraile (The Monk). If you look carefully, you may (just) see a resemblance to a praying monk.

Off to the right, a road wriggles round a reservoir, the Presa de los Hornos. Not far away is the **Degollada de Bercerra** (daily

10am–5pm; free), an information centre with a *mirador* offering panoramic views. Looming above is the **Pico de las Nieves** ㉗, the highest peak on the island, crowned by a radar station and tv transmitter. The summit is not accessible as it is used as a military base, but there is a lookout point not far below.

The road to the west from Ayacata, signposted to Bentaiga, is asphalted at first but soon becomes a gravel track. After Roque Nublo, **Roque Bentaiga** is the most spectacular monolith in the range. In 1483, it was the site of a fierce battle in which the Spaniards, led by Pedro de Vera, defeated the Guanches. A Guanche refuge, called the Cueva del Rey (King's Cave), lies at the foot of the outcrop. It is well worth stopping at the **Centro de Interpretación** (daily 10am–4pm, Sat–Sun until 6pm; hours unpredictable in winter) to get some background information. From here, those with enough energy can scramble the last stretch to the peak.

CAMINOS REALES

A series of ancient paths known as *caminos reales* – royal paths – has been restored and opened up to walkers as part of an attempt to promote conservation-conscious tourism and *senderismo* – hiking. These old tracks, once the only means of navigating the interior of Gran Canaria, centre on Cruz de Tejeda and radiate out to much of the island, from Maspalomas in the south to Agaete in the northwest. While some walks are demanding, others are relatively short and gentle. For more information, contact the Turismo de Gran Canaria, Calle Triana 93, Las Palmas (tel: 928 219 600), or visit the helpful government bookshop, the Librería del Cabildo Insular, Calle Cano 24, Las Palmas (tel: 928 381 539; www.libroscanarios.org) for maps and books in English.

FORTALEZA GRANDE AND SANTA LUCÍA

An alternative way to approach the central peaks is from the east, from Agüimes, via Santa Lucía on the GC-550 or from the Cruce de Sardina exit off the motorway (GC-65). It almost goes without saying that these are winding roads with sharp bends, but the scenery is spectacular, with prickly pears, euphorbia and olive trees gradually losing ground to bare, reddish rock.

Off to the left of the GC-65, you will see **Fortaleza Grande**, a rock uncannily shaped like a castle, which was one of the last refuges of the Guanches. Some of those who survived the defeat at Roque Bentaiga obeyed the command of their leader, Tenesor Semidan, to surrender; others, it is said, threw themselves from these cliffs.

Surrounded by pines, **Santa Lucía** ❷ is a beautiful little village with blindingly white houses, bougainvillaea tumbling over walls, and an imposing domed church with a double belltower. There's a children's playground and a small museum, the **Museo Castillo de la Fortaleza** (daily 10.30am–5pm) where Guanche artefacts, agricultural tools and a Roman amphora are displayed.

A final way to approach the peaks is via Moya or Arucas in the north. The road from Arucas is the better of the two, but the Moya route wends past the lovely Pinos de Gáldar pine forest. Both lead – circuitously, of course – to Cruz de Tejeda.

Gran Canaria has excellent conditions for windsurfing

THINGS TO DO

SPORTS

The spectrum of sports and outdoor activities available on Gran Canaria runs from the mildly energetic to the extremely vigorous. While most of the activities take place on, in or under the water, there are many land-based pursuits, from hiking to horse riding and golf.

WINDSURFING

Gran Canaria is considered one of the best places in the world for windsurfing – some say only Hawaii beats it. It can be practised all along the coast, from Melenera in the east through to Maspalomas in the south. At **Playa de Vargas** and **Pozo Izquierdo** near Arinaga, strong winds are constant all year round and waves always high. A little further south, near San Agustín, winds are good in Bahía Feliz and Playa del Águila. The two best windsurf schools, which offer beginner and advanced courses, are **Fanatic Boarders Center** (Playa de Trajalillo, Urbanización Bahía Feliz; www.fbcgrancanaria.com) and **BD Surf School** (Playa del Águila, San Agustín and Playa del Ingles; tel: 928 767 999, www.surfbd.com), run by record-holding 42-time world champion Björn Dunkerbeck. Windsurfing conditions are also decent on the Playa de las Canteras, Las Palmas and at Gáldar in the far northwest corner.

SURFING AND BODYBOARDING

The north of the island, between Las Palmas and Gáldar, is best for surfing and bodyboarding. Constant onshore winds along this rocky coastline make ideal conditions for surfers, and waves can reach up to 5m (16ft) high. Conditions are also good around Arinaga, on the east coast, and between Playa del Inglés and

Diving into the underwater playground

Maspalomas in the south, where tuition and courses are offered by **PR Surfing** (Av. de Moya no. 6, C.C Eurocenter loc 80, Maspolomas; tel: 628 104 025, www.prsurfing.com).

DIVING

There is a fascinating world beneath the waters off Gran Canaria and a number of excellent diving sites. In Las Palmas, where La Barra forms a giant aquarium, protected from the force of the waves, there is a wealth of underwater marine life to explore. On the east coast at **Playa del Cabrón**, the diversity of fish and vegetation is so great that the area has been designated a marine reserve. **Pasito Blanco**, in the south near **Puerto Rico**, is another good spot, with ideal conditions for underwater photography, and there are two wrecks off this coast that are ripe for exploration (experienced divers only). In the northwest, **Sardina** is a popular spot for night dives into rocky depths of 17m (52ft).

SPORTS

Reputable diving schools with qualified instructors include: **Buceo Canarias Medusasub** (Calle Joaquin Blanco Torrent opposite dock H, Las Palmas; tel: 928 232 085, www.buceocanarias.com); **Zeus Dive Center** (Hotel IFA Continental, Av Italia 2, Playa del Ingles; tel: 689 082 298, www.zeusdivecenter.com); **Davy Jones Diving** (Calle Luis Velasco 36-38, Playa de Arinaga, Aguimes; tel: 928 180 840, www.davyjonesdiving.com); and **Gran Canaria Divers** (Calle la Puntillo 3; tel: 928 948 424, www.grancanariadivers.com). Free pick-up and drop-off between accommodation and dive sites is often included in the price.

SAILING

Gran Canaria is a sailor's dream, especially from April to October. Winds are reliable, and the climate is excellent. The main centres are Las Palmas and the south coast, specifically Pasito Blanco, Arguineguín, Puerto Rico and Puerto de Mogán. The island attracts experienced sailors – members of Puerto Rico's sailing school have brought home several Olympic gold medals – but it suits beginners too.

The annual Atlantic Rally for Cruisers (ARC; www.worldcruising.com) kicks off at the Muelle Deportivo in Las Palmas in Gran Canaria and embarks on the mighty 2700-nautical mile journey to St Lucia in the Caribbean.

Boat trips

To experience the sea while someone else does the work, take a trip in a glass bottom boat run by Líneas Salmon (tel: 649 919 383, www.lineassalmon.es) or Líneas Bluebird (tel: 629 989 633/366, www.lineasbluebird.com) between the ports of Arguineguín, Puerto Rico and Puerto de Mogán. Or try the Afrikat from Puerto Rico (tel: 637 564 679, www.afrikat.com) for a lazy day on a sailing catamaran, with on-board food and drink.

Keen sailors flock to the south coast

Among many reliable sailing clubs and schools are: **Real Club Náutico**, Calle León y Castillo 308, Las Palmas, tel: 928 234 566, www.rcngc.com; **Real Club Victoria**, Paseo de las Canteras 4, tel: 928 460 630, www.realclubvictoria.com; **AIS TraC**, Juan Deniz 10, Puerto Mogan, tel: 622 170 018, www.aistrac.com; and the **ICI-Sailing Club**, Calle Leon y Castillo 308, tel: 407 501 014, www.ici-sailing.org. For information on lateen sailing, contact the **Federación de Vela Latina Canaria**, Muelle Deportivo, Las Palmas, tel: 928 230 616, www.federacionvelalatinadebotes.com.

DEEP-SEA FISHING

Gran Canaria is well known for its game fishing, and Pasito Blanco, Puerto Rico and Puerto de Mogán are the major centres. Puerto Rico's fishermen are the proud holders of numerous world records in deep-sea fishing, but this is a sport in which beginners can take part too. Several varieties of tuna and marlin as well as swordfish and sometimes sharks can be found in these well-stocked waters. The deep-sea fishing season is roughly from May to September, but there is bottom-fishing available all year round.

A number of organizations offer fishing trips that include lunch and equipment; try **White Striker** (Puerto Rico; tel: 610 480 760, www.whitestriker.com) with a knowledgeable skipper. Those who don't want to fish can relax on the solarium at the front of the boat. Tuna is sold direct to restaurants; marlin is collected by staff from a children's home in Las Palmas. Also recommended in Puerto Rico is **Cavalier & Blue Marlin 3** (tel: 607 626 237, www.bluemarlin3.com).

WALKING

There's lots to do on land, and the most popular activity is hiking – *senderismo*. This is being promoted by the Cabildo Insular as a way of diversifying the tourist industry and encouraging visitors to explore the interior of the island. More than 66,000 hectares (164,000 acres) of land in Gran Canaria is under a protection order.

ANCIENT SPORTS

Lucha Canaria – Canary Islands wrestling – is the most popular traditional sport on the islands and can be seen at rural fiestas, in the Estadio López Socas in Las Palmas, and in Gáldar. Two teams of twelve wrestlers take it in turns to face a member of the opposing team in a sandy ring, with the aim of throwing the opponent to the ground. After a maximum of three rounds (*bregas*), the winner is the team that loses the fewest wrestlers. The game was practised in pre-Hispanic times, when it may have had more serious overtones.

Juego del palo (stick fighting) is another ancient rural sport, also practised at fiestas. The object is to move the body as little as possible while attacking and fending off the blows of an opponent.

Real Club de Golf de Las Palmas

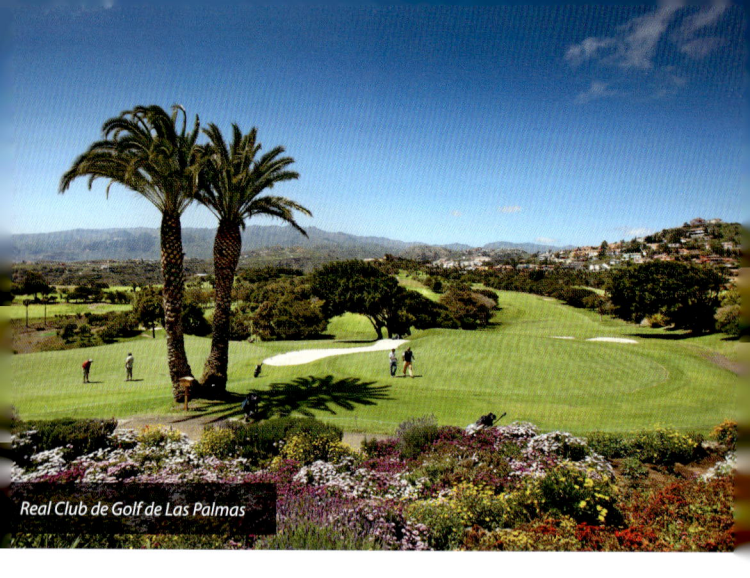

There are rural parks, nature reserves, fully protected reserves and natural monuments, with most of this land accessible to the public. A series of ancient paths, the *caminos reales*, or royal paths (see page 80), once the only means of traversing much of the island, has been opened up for walkers. There are challenging walks and climbs in the mountainous centre of the island, but there are many other less strenuous routes as well.

A guidebook to these paths can be purchased in the bookshop of the **Cabildo Insular de Gran Canaria** (Calle Cano 24, Las Palmas). Alternatively, contact the Turismo de Gran Canaria (Calle Triana 93, Las Palmas; tel: 928 219 600, www.grancanaria.com), which publishes a series of leaflets, including maps.

There are many great walks in the *barrancos*. For general information on organized hikes, contact **Grupo Montañero Gran Canaria** (Calle Guillermo Santana Rivero 1, Las Palmas; tel: 928 427 475, www.gmgrancanaria.es). For hikes with a knowledgeable guide, contact **Hiking World** (Plaza Tiscamanita, Maspolomas; tel: 654 588 038, www.hikingworldgrancanaria.com). Visit www.visitaguimes.com for walking routes and trails in the Barranco de Guayadeque and other suggested routes.

Whether you are in a group or not, remember the basics: strong, comfortable shoes, sunblock, sun hat, sweater or jacket for lower temperatures in the mountains, and something to cover exposed shoulders in the sun. Take plenty of drinking water with you – it's easy to get dehydrated in the heat of the day.

GOLF

There are eight golf courses in Gran Canaria: three in the north, five in the south. They include the **Real Club de Golf de Las Palmas** (Santa Brígida; tel: 928 351 050, make online reservations at www.realclubdegolfdelaspalmas.com) with 18 holes, par 71. It is draped across the rim of the Bandama volcanic crater and is the oldest club in Spain, founded by British expatriates in 1891. **Maspalomas Golf Club** (Avenida TTOO Neckermann s/n; tel: 928 762 581, www.maspalomasgolf.net) has 18 holes, par 73, and has also been operating for some years. **Salobre Golf Club** (Autopista gc-1, Km53 between Maspalomas and Puerto de Mogán; tel: 928 943 000, www.salobrehotel.com) has two excellent courses (new and old). For more information, visit the island's official website, www.grancanaria.com.

HORSE RIDING

The **Real Club de Golf** at Santa Brígida (tel: 928 351 050, www.realclubdegolfdelaspalmas.com) has a riding school. Lessons and trekking are also available at the **Picadero Oasis de Maspalomas** (tel: 928 762 378) and **El Salobre Canyon Horse Farm** (Maspaloma; tel: 616 418 363, www.elsalobrehr.es), which arranges pick-ups from the southern resorts.

FLYING, PARACHUTING AND SKY DIVING

Test your mettle with a flying or parachuting session. Contact the **Escuela Canaria de Parapente** (tel: 626 331 588, www.parapentegrancanaria.com), or the **Club de Parapente Sirocco** (tel: 696 860 216) in Las Palmas. For sky diving – a flight over the Maspalomas dunes and a jump in tandem with an instructor from 3000m (9840ft) – contact **Paraclub Gran Canaria** (tel: 928 157 000, www.iJump.es).

JEEP AND QUAD SAFARIS

Jeep safaris from Playa del Inglés to Fataga are popular. Most include a barbecue lunch in the price; some throw in a free video of your trip, others will sell you one. Try **Discovery Jeep Safari** (tel: 928 775 188, www.discoverysafari.es). Quad safaris are for the daring. They head off-road on the route to Fataga, bouncing along riverbeds and rocky tracks. Contact **Free-Motion** (www.free-motion.com), which also organizes more easy-going bike tours and rents mountain bikes.

SHOPPING

Gran Canaria looks set to maintain its status as a Free Trade Zone for the foreseeable future, despite membership of the EU, and taxes (IGIC) are low, at seven percent, so there are savings to be made on tobacco, spirits, perfume, cosmetics, watches, jewellery, and electronic and optical equipment in Las Palmas duty-free shops.

Handicraft items (*artesanía*), including textiles, baskets and ceramics, can be found in shops and markets all over the island, but the best-quality goods are sold in the outlets of the **Fundación para la Etnografía y el Desarrollo de la Artesanía Canaria** (FEDAC; www.fedac.org). These are situated at Calle Domingo J. Navarro 7, Las Palmas, tel: 928 369 661, and in the tourist office in Maspolomas lighthouse, tel: 928 772 445. The FEDAC shops also sell the small knives once used by banana workers and shepherds, which have since become collectors' items. These *cuchillos canarios* or *naifes* have a wide blade and a goat horn handle decorated with inlaid patterns.

Unusual plants

The Gando airport shop has a wide selection of plants, from miniature dragon trees to *strelitzia* (bird of paradise) flowers, as well as a variety of seeds. Whether or not they will grow in the English climate is a gamble, but they make unusual gifts – and there is no restriction on bringing them into the UK.

Calle Peregrina, just round the corner from FEDAC in Las Palmas, is peppered with attractive little boutiques and art galleries. The **Librería del Cabildo Insular** (the official government bookshop; Calle Cano 24, Las Palmas; tel: 928 381 539, www.libroscanarios.org) is the best place to find maps and books about all the Canary Islands. In the big commercial zones of Las Palmas, you will find all the major stores, Spanish and international. The biggest centres in and around Las Palmas are **Las Arenas** near the Auditorio Kraus; **La Ballena** in the upper town; and the biggest Spanish department store, **El Corte Inglés** in the **Avenida Mesa y López**, which is known as a 'zona comercial'. Another centre, with a range of shops as well as cafés, restaurants, cinemas and discos, is **El Muelle**, on the Muelle Santa Catalina.

Among edible items, *queso de flor*, the famous cheese made in Guía, is a good choice. The cheeses can be tasted and bought at the Santa María Guía factory and at farmers' markets around the island. Jars of *mojo* sauce in many varieties and *bienmesabe* (the syrupy almond dessert) are widely available. **La Elvira** (Calle Juan Ramón Giménez 45, Mercado de Altavista puesto 15, Las Palmas; tel: 662 323 608) sells good-quality island wines as well as local and Latin American foods.

MARKETS

Most towns have a weekly market, selling food, flowers and household goods. There's a good one in **Puerto de Mogán** (Friday and

A colourful stall at Vegueta food market

Monday) and another in the San Fernando district of **Playa del Inglés** (Wednesday and Saturday). **San Mateo** has a huge farmers' market on Sunday morning. In Las Palmas, the slightly overpriced **Vegueta** food market is a riot of colours and scents every morning except Sunday, and is surrounded by tiny white-tiled bars. Head to **Mercado del Puerto** (Calle Albareda; open daily) for a great variety of fresh vegetables, fruits, meats and fish at bargain prices.

NIGHTLIFE

Discos, clubs and bars rapidly fall in and out of favour. Very little happens before midnight, so a quiet place you pass at 10.30pm may be popping two hours later. In Las Palmas, Plaza de España in the Mesa y López district is lively. **Ginger** on Paseo de las Canteras is the perfect place to sit outside with a mojito looking over the beach. **Bar La Buena Vida**, on Calle Ripoche, a stone's throw from Parque Santa Catalina, may be a small drinking den but it's big on hospitality – and a local favourite.

Further south, the café tables in Plaza Hurtado de Mendoza are full till the early hours. **La Azotea de Benito** (www.lazoteadebenito.com), on Plaza de Hurtado Mendoza 1, boasts excellent cocktails and wonderful views from its roof terrace. **Chester** (Calle Simon Bolivar 3) also serves good cocktails.

There are hundreds of bars, clubs and discos in Playa del Inglés and Maspalomas. Flyers handed out in the street or listings in local papers will point the way. The commercial centres are the places to find most options. **Chinawhite** in Maspalomas (Avenida de Espana 7; www.chinawhitegrancanaria.com) is popular and has a good rota of international DJs. A firm favourite, **Iguazú Lounge** in Playa des Ingles (Avenida Tirajana) is a stylish bar with a reputation for serving some of the best cocktails in the area. The **Yumbo Centre** is known for its gay bars and clubs (www.yumbocentrum.com).

For a flutter, try Casino Las Palmas in Las Palmas (Calle Simon Bolivar 3; tel: 928 234 882, www.casinolaspalmas.com) or the Gran Casino in Meloneras (Calle Mar Mediterráneo 1; tel: 928 143 909, www.grancasinocostameloneras.com). Dress smartly and don't forget your passport.

From casinos to classical, the **Auditorio Alfredo Kraus** at the far end of Playa de las Canteras (www.auditorioteatrolaspalmasgc.es) presents excellent music recitals by the resident Las Palmas Philharmonic and visiting orchestras, and performances by top-class soloists.

The **Teatro Cuyás** (Calle Viera y Clavijo s/n, Triana; www.teatrocuyas.com) stages world and classical music, dance and theatre, as does the **Teatro Pérez Galdós** (Plaza Stagno 1; www.auditorioteatrolaspalmasgc.es). **CICCA** (Alameda de Colón 1; tel: 928 368 687, www.lacajadecanarias.es) has a varied programme of films, music, modern dance and theatre.

CHILDREN'S GRAN CANARIA

Gran Canaria is a great place for children as there are numerous places to entertain them when they tire of the beach or the sun gets too intense. Close to Playa del Inglés/Maspalomas, and with regular bus services, you will find:

Mundo Aborigen (daily 9am–6pm), Parque Rural de Ayagaures, Carretera de Fataga Km6, tel: 928 172 295. A great recreation of a Guanche settlement, with life-size models. Adults usually enjoy it as much as kids do.

Camel Safari Park (Mon–Sat 9am–5pm), La Baranda, Carretera de Fataga, tel: 928 798 680, www.camelsafarigrancanaria.com. Camel treks, a shop and a restaurant are on offer here.

Aqualand (daily 10am–5pm), Carretera Palmitos Park Km3, tel: 928 140 525, www.aqualand.es. The biggest waterpark in the

Canaries, with pools, slides, flumes and water attractions of all descriptions.

Holiday World (daily 4–11pm), Maspalomas, tel: 928 730 498, www.holidayworldmaspalomas.com. Another huge leisure park.

Sioux City (Tues–Sun 10am–5pm, plus Fri barbecue 8pm), Cañon del Águila, San Agustín, tel: 928 762 573, www.parquetematicosiouxcitypark.com. A fun-filled Wild West theme park, complete with gunfights and bank hold-ups.

Submarine Adventure (daily 10am–5pm), Puerto de Mogán, tel: 928 565 108, www.atlantidasubmarine.com. A 90-minute voyage to the bottom of the sea in a yellow submarine.

Cocodrilo Park (Fri–Sun 10.30am–4.30pm, daily at peak times), Los Corralillos, Agüimes, tel: 928 784 725, www.cocodriloparkzoo.com. Wildlife includes parrots, monkeys and deer, as well as around three hundred crocodiles.

Guagua Turística (daily), Las Palmas. Children usually enjoy a trip around town on the open-topped tourist bus. You can hop on and off all day at places of interest.

Museo Elder (Tues–Thurs 9.30am–7.30pm, Fri–Sun 10am–8pm), www.museoelder.org. The big science and technology museum in Parque Santa Catalina, is a hit with children thanks to its hands-on activities and a section especially designed for very young ones, as well as an IMAX cinema.

WHAT'S ON

6 January: Epifanía del Señor (Epiphany). Children receive their Christmas presents. In Las Palmas the Three Kings (Los Reyes) ride into town, sometimes on camels, throwing sweets to the crowd.

February: Fiesta de Almendros (Almond Blossom Festival) in Tejeda and Valsequillo (date varies). Traditional handicrafts, dance performances and sports displays.

Late February/early March: Carnival. Celebrations are particularly outrageous in Las Palmas and Playa del Inglés.

April: Semana Santa. The week preceding Easter is a time of solemn processions. Also International Film Festival in Las Palmas, various locations.

End April to early May: Cheese festival, Santa María de Guía. Traditional dancing and lots of local produce.

Mid-June: Corpus Christi. The streets of Vegueta and the Plaza de Santa Ana in Las Palmas, and main squares in Arucas and Gáldar, are carpeted with flowers, grasses and coloured sand.

24 June: San Juan (Feast of St John). Dancing, processions and sporting activities in Artenara, Telde, Las Palmas and Arucas.

16 July: Nuestra Señora del Carmen, the patron saint of fishermen, is honoured in all ports, but especially in Arguineguín and Puerto de Mogán. Statues of the Virgin are taken out to sea in colourful processions of decorated boats.

4 August: Bajada de las Ramas (Bringing down the Branches) is held in Agaete and Puerto de las Nieves. The villagers carry branches from the mountains to the sea and whip the waves.

8 September: Virgen del Pino. Important festival in Teror, which is a mixture of religious rituals and secular fun.

11 September: Fiesta del Charco (Festival of the Lagoon) in Puerto de la Aldea, San Nicolás. Participants try to catch fish with their hands, and duck each other into the water.

Second Saturday in October: Fiestas de la Naval (Festival of the Sea). Maritime processions in Las Palmas and other ports celebrate the victory of the Armada over the English in 1595.

FOOD AND DRINK

Canary Islands' cuisine has much in common with that of mainland Spain's, but it is infused with interesting regional differences. There are also dishes similar to those found in parts of Latin America – although whether these recipes were introduced by Canarian emigrants, or American inventions brought back by returnees, is debatable.

You will also find many restaurants where the cooking is described as *cocina vasca* (Basque) or *cocina gallega* (Galician) because a number of cooks from these northern regions of Spain have opened restaurants on the island. These two regions have a reputation for some of the finest cooking in Spain so they are a much-welcomed addition to the culinary landscape of Gran Canaria.

FISH

As you would expect on an Atlantic island, there is an abundance of fish and seafood on restaurant menus. Along with the ubiquitous *sardinas*, fresh from the ocean, the fish most commonly chalked up on blackboards are *cherne* (sea bass), *vieja* (parrot fish), *sama* (sea bream) and *bacalao* (salt cod). You will also find *merluza* (hake) *atún* (tuna) and *bonito* (a variety of tuna) and seafood such as *gambas* (prawns), *pulpo* (octopus), *calamares* (squid) and *almejas* (clams).

Often, fish will be served simply grilled along with salad, *mojo* sauce and *papas arrugadas* – a perfectly balanced dish – but there are numerous other ways that it may appear on your table. *Sancocho canario* is a popular recipe, a stew made with red grouper or sea bass, potatoes and yams, spiced up with a hot variety of *mojo*. *Salpicón de pescado* is another dish you will see on many menus: this is sea bass or grouper cooked, chopped and served cold with a mixture of onions, garlic, tomatoes and peppers, topped with crumbled hard-boiled egg and olives. A delicacy introduced from the Basque country is *calamares rellenos de bacalao* – small squid with a tasty, cod-based stuffing, sometimes served in a creamy sauce.

Local tapas plates

MEAT

If you don't like fish, don't despair, there's plenty of meat to be found. *Cabrito* (kid) – sometimes called *baifo* – and *conejo* (rabbit) are most common, but pork (*cerdo*) and chicken (*pollo*) are popular. There are also some good steaks to be had in restaurants catering to tourists. Both goat and rabbit are often served *al salmorejo* (with green peppers, in a herb and garlic marinade). *Chorizo*, the red spicy sausage found all over Spain, also crops up in a variety of guises.

SOUPS

Most of the world's traditional dishes originated as a way of filling stomachs with what was available and inexpensive. In the Canary Islands, this meant a whole range of substantial soups and stews. *Ropa vieja* ("old clothes") is a mixture of meat, tomatoes and chickpeas; *puchero* includes meat, pumpkin and any vegetables available; while *rancho canario* – mixing vermicelli with chickpeas, potatoes, bacon, chorizo and chicken – is the most elaborate and some say the best. Many of the soups contain chunks of corn on the cob. Vegetarians should note that even watercress soup (*potaje de berros*), a staple of many menus, has chunks of bacon in it. And celery soup (*potaje de apio*) may contain scraps of pork.

VEGETABLES

The vegetables you are offered will be those that are in season and because the island does not produce a great variety, and imports are expensive, choice may be limited. Pulses such as lentils (*lentejas*) and chickpeas (*garbanzos*) bulk out many recipes. Canary tomatoes are delicious; look out for *tomates aliñados*, tomato salad drizzled with olive oil and lashings of garlic. *Pimientos de padrón* – small green peppers cooked whole and studded with salt – originated in Galicia and are now found everywhere. Avocados (strictly speaking a fruit, not a vegetable) are served at a perfect stage of ripeness.

The ubiquitous pimientos de padrón

Most dishes contain or are accompanied by potatoes (*papas*), and sometimes by *ñame*, a kind of yam. You'll encounter *papas arrugadas* (wrinkled potatoes), which are served with meat and fish or by themselves as tapas. They are small potatoes – the yellow-fleshed Tenerife variety are best – cooked in their skins in salted water then dried over a low heat until their skins wrinkle and a salty crust forms. It is said that this dish originated with fishermen who used to boil the potatoes in seawater.

MOJO

Papas arrugadas, and many meat dishes, are usually accompanied by *mojo rojo*, a sauce whose basic ingredients are tomatoes, peppers and paprika. A spicier version (*mojo picón*) contains hot chili pepper as well. *Mojo verde* is a green sauce made with oil, vinegar, garlic, coriander and parsley, usually served with fish. The sauces arrive at the table in small bowls so you can use as much or as little as you like. Every restaurant – and probably every home – seems to have their own version and entire *mojo* recipe books are published.

GOFIO

Made of wheat, barley or a mixture of the two, *gofio* was the staple food of the Guanches and still forms an essential part of the island diet today – you even see sacks of *gofio para perros* (*gofio* for dogs). The cereal is toasted before being ground into flour, and has a multiplicity of uses. It is stirred into soups and into children's milk and used to thicken sauces. It is whipped into ice cream and mixed with oil, salt and sugar into a kind of bread, not unlike *polenta*. It is also blended with fish stock to make a thick soup called *gofio escaldado*.

CHEESE, FRUIT AND DESSERTS

There are only a few Canary Island cheeses, but they are delicious. The best known is a soft cheese, *queso de flor*, which is made in Guía using a mixture of sheep and cows' milk curdled with the juice of flowers from the cardoon thistle and has been awarded a Denomination of Origin. It has also won several World Cheese Awards, as has the *queso tierno de Valsequillo*, a mild, smooth cheese like mozzarella.

Home-grown Canary fruit is delicious. As well as the small, local bananas, there are papayas, guavas, mangoes and oranges, delicious by themselves, squeezed into fresh juices or used to flavour ice cream. On many menus, desserts are limited to ice cream (*helado*), *flan* (the ubiquitous caramel custard), fruit platters, and the one you see everywhere, *bienmesabe*, which translates

Truchas canarias

Trucha is a word to be careful with. It actually means trout, but *truchas canarias* are almond and aniseed doughnuts, one of the most popular sweet snacks.

as 'tastes good to me' – and so it does. There are numerous recipes, but basically it is a mixture of crushed almonds, lemon, sugar, cinnamon and egg yolks.

WHAT TO DRINK

The breakfast drink of choice is coffee. *Café solo* is a small, strong black, like an *espresso*; a *cortado*, served in a glass, is a shot of coffee with a small amount of hot milk; *café con leche* is a large, milky coffee. An *Americano* is a shot of coffee with added hot water. Hot chocolate is sometimes available for breakfast, but if you ask for tea, you will just get a teabag in a little pot.

You are advised not to drink tap water, but *agua mineral* is sold everywhere – *con gas* is sparkling, *sin gas* still. *Zumo de naranja*, freshly squeezed orange juice, is widely available and in some bars and cafés you can get more exotic concoctions.

Wine is usually drunk with meals, most of it imported from the mainland; Rioja is one of the favourites. There are many wineries on Gran Canaria, which has a recently introduced Denomination of Origin (DOC), but they come nowhere near to supplying demand. Monte Lentiscal, which has its own DOC, is the most widely available local wine. Tenerife is a bigger producer, but its wines are not regularly found in restaurants.

When Arucas had a thriving sugar industry, it also used to be a centre of rum production. There is still a distillery there, the

Destileria Arehucas (www.arehucas.es), producing excellent rum, but sugar has to be imported now so the output is greatly reduced. Rum forms the basis of *Mejunje*, a local drink in which the spirit is blended with honey and lemon. Another speciality is *Guindilla*, the cherry liqueur made in San Bartolomé.

Beer is extremely popular on the island. You will see familiar Spanish brands such as San Miguel, and other imported beers are also available, but the most popular thirst-quencher is the locally produced Tropical.

WHERE TO EAT

When it comes to places to eat, the choice is wide. There are upmarket restaurants in Las Palmas and Maspalomas that can compete with those in any capital city and are not expensive by northern European standards. There are fishermen's *tavernas* where the fish is likely to be fresh and wholesome, with few trimmings; and rural *parrillas* – grills – where all kinds of meat and sausage are barbecued over an open fire and dished up with generous helpings of *papas arrugadas* and *mojo rojo*.

A *piscolabis* is a snack bar serving a variety of little sandwiches and snacks. When you see restaurants advertising *cocina casalinga* – home-cooking – you'll get inexpensive, typically Canarian food, although the quality, of course, can vary. There are not many places that style themselves as tapas bars, but many middle-of-the-range and inexpensive restaurants will offer a selection of tapas, and some of the portions are quite large – two or three would make a meal for most people.

Bars, generally, are places in which to drink, not eat, although most will have croissants or pastries to accompany the morning coffee; some may serve sandwiches (*bocadillos*) or a limited range of tapas. A *kiosco* has the same role and can be found in the main squares of most towns and villages.

WHEN TO EAT

The islanders, like the people of mainland Spain, eat late. It is not unusual to sit down to lunch at three o'clock, and ten o'clock is a relatively early hour to start dinner. Some restaurants may close for a few hours between lunch and dinner, but many serve food all day. Those who cater mostly to foreign visitors, aware that habits are different, will have their lunch menus out by midday and serve dinner as early as you like.

Sunday lunch is a major event in Gran Canaria and as this continues throughout the afternoon many restaurants are closed on Sunday evening. Some also close one evening during the week. Because the high season runs between November and April, and restaurateurs need to take a holiday, some close completely for three or four weeks in mid-summer.

Locals typically eat dinner after 10pm

TO HELP YOU ORDER

Could we have a table, please? **¿Nos puede dar una mesa, por favor?**
Do you have a set menu? **¿Tiene un menú del día?**
I would like... **Quisiera…**
The bill, please **La cuenta, por favor**

MENU READER

à la plancha grilled
agua mineral mineral water
al ajillo in garlic
almejas clams
arroz rice
asado roast
atún tuna
azúcar sugar
bacalao cod
bocadillo sandwich
boquerones anchovies
buey/res beef
cabrito kid
calamares squid
callos tripe
cangrejo crab
cerdo pork
cerveza beer
champiñones mushrooms
cocido stew
conejo rabbit
cordero lamb
ensalada salad
entremeses hors d'oeuvre
flan caramel custard
helado ice cream
jamón serrano cured ham
judías beans
langosta lobster
leche milk
mariscos shellfish
mejillones mussels
morcilla black pudding
pan bread
pescado fish
picante spicy
poco hecho rare
pollo chicken
postre dessert
pulpitos baby octopus
queso cheese
sal salt
salsa sauce
ternera veal
tortilla omelette
trucha trout
verduras vegetables
vino wine

WHERE TO EAT

We have used the following symbols to give an idea of the price for a three-course meal for one, including wine, cover and service:

€€€€ over 60 euros
€€€ 40–60 euros
€€ 25–40 euros
€ below 25 euros

LAS PALMAS

De Contrabando €€€ *Calle Fernando Guanarteme 16, tel: 928 228 416,* www.decontrabandorestaurante.com. Innovative fusion cuisine with influences from around the world, served in an elegant Gatsby-style dining space. The dishes are perfect for sharing. Good selection of Canarian wines.

Deliciosa Marta €€€ *Perez Galdos, 23, Las Palmas, tel: 928 370 882.* Arguably the best restaurant in Las Palmas: great food, friendly staff and a lovely romantic ambience. Lamb shoulder and steak tartare are both highly recommended. Advance booking essential.

El Cerdo Que Ríe €€ *Paseo de las Canteras 31, tel: 928 271 731.* Established in the 1960s when northern European tourists first came to Las Palmas, the Danish-owned '*Laughing Pig*' is still extremely popular with visitors. Its large menu, written up outside the restaurant, has strong though not exclusive Scandinavian leanings.

El Deseo €€ *Calle Medizábal 23, tel: 640 773 723,* www.eldeseolaspalmas.es. Close to the Vegueta market, this cosy restaurant serves up delicious and authentic Canarian cooking in a relaxed and friendly atmosphere. The baby quid in green *mojo* is particularly delicious. It also has a good-value set tapas menu. Closed Mon.

El Padrino €€€ *Calle Jesús Nazareno 1, tel: 928 462 094,* www.restaurantelpadrino.es. This fish restaurant on La Isleta is famous not only for its seafood specialities, but also for marvellous views. Eat indoors or outside in a kind of marquee. Recommended for Sunday lunch, when it is wise to book.

El Patio del Cuyás €€ *Teatro Cuyás, Calle Viero y Clavijo s/n, Triana, tel: 928 384 800, www.teatrocuyas.com.* Part of a theatre in Triana, *El Patio* serves up good food prepared by a well-regarded young chef who draws on culinary influences from the different corners of northern Spain in which he has worked. Book for lunch. Closed Mon, Tues and Wed evenings and all day Sun.

Embarcadero €€€ *Club Marítimo Varadero, Muelle Deportivo, tel: 928 233 067, www.restauranteembarcadero.com.* In this smart waterfront restaurant, the scallops with asparagus and smoked Hierro cheese is one of the star turns. Great location and good choice of wines.

Lupe €€ *Calle Dr Miguel Rosas 16, tel: 928 229 603.* Unpretentious tapas haunt with an interesting menu and attentive service. Expect inventive dishes like cod confit in sea sauce, squid and prawns or tuna tataki battered in sesame with sautéed vegetables and teriyaki sauce. Do not leave without trying the perfectly baked cheesecakes. Closed Mon.

La Marinera €€€ *Alonso Ojeda, Paseo de las Canteras La Puntilla, tel: 928 461 555/928 468 802, www.restaurantelamarineralaspalmas.com.* At the end of Playa de las Canteras, this restaurant has a dining room so close to the sea that you could almost reach out and catch the fish yourself. Fortunately, they do it for you, and cook it extremely well. Barbecued meats are also on offer, as are local Canary Island wines.

Ribera del Río Miño €€€ *Calle Oluf Palme, 21, Las Palmas, tel: 928 264 431, www.riberadelriomino.com.* A pricey but popular restaurant close to Playa de las Canteras and Plaza España. Recommended for its Galician cuisine and good wines.

Rincon de Triana €€€ *Calle José Franchy Roca 59, tel: 634 680 614, www.rincondetriana.es.* The Spanish and Mediterranean cooking here never ceases to impress. Everything is delicious, from the tuna tartare to the aubergines wrapped in dough with honey. Not to mention the desserts, which include an incredible chocolate coulant. Ask for a table on the outdoor terrace facing Las Canteras Beach.

THE EAST

Agüimes

Restaurant El Guachinche €€ *Calle Doctor Joaquín Artiles, tel: 626 201 872*. Situated near the historic centre, this is a fabulous place to taste authentic Canarian cuisine – the roasted cheese is extremely good. Reserve a table in advance if you want a much-coveted spot on the terrace. Closed Mon–Wed, plus Thurs and Sun evenings.

Santa Brígida

Bodegón Vandama €€€ *Carretera Bandama, 116, tel: 928 352 754*, www.bodegonvandama.com. This charming tavern is off the beaten track – and all the better for it. Surrounded by vineyards and gardens, its speciality is the *parrilla* (grilled meats) served with tasty salsas, pimienta or Roquefort, and a glass of house wine. Closed all day Mon–Tues, and Sun evenings.

Telde

La Rubia €€ *Calle Luis Morote, 47, tel: 928 132 223*. Arguably the best seafood restaurant in Telde, and therefore often gets very busy. Do not be deterred by the decor, as the food is excellent and the choice of *mariscos* (seafood) amazing. It's good value too. No bookings. Closed Nov.

THE SOUTH

Maspalomas

La Casa Vieja €€ *Calle el Lomo 139, Carretera de Fataga, tel: 928 077 891*. Under new ownership since 2021, this iconic rustic restaurant has been refurbished and is now a perfect mix of traditional and modern decor. The food too is classic with a contemporary spin. Closed Mon.

Ceniza Restaurante €€€ *Paseo Boulevard El Faro, tel: 686 874 202,* www.cenizarestaurante.com. Right on the waterfront promenade, *Ceniza* offers fine dining with a Spanish twist in a chic, contemporary space. The dishes are beautifully presented, and the flavours distinctive. The catch of the day is a popular choice, which could include seabass or turbot.

La Proa Casa Reyes Meloneras €€ *Centro Comercial Meloneras Playa, Local 103, tel: 928 142 403*. This smart restaurant, with its excellent location and fantastic sea views, is also great value for money. The fresh fish and seafood is the highlight here.

Samsara €€ *Avenida del Oasis 30, Maspalomas, tel: 928 142 736,* www.samsara-gc.com. This Asian fusion restaurant is an ideal location for a romantic evening; highlights include the tuna and duck *carpaccio*. Advance booking recommended. Closed Mon.

Mogán

Acaymo €€ *Calle los Pasitos 21, tel: 928 569 263*, www.restauranteacaymogan.es. This former village school has been reimagined as an attractive rustic restaurant, serving traditional island dishes, fish stews and roast meats with *mojo* sauce. Closed Tues.

Casa Enrique €€ *Calle San José 3, tel: 928 569 542*. Big, rather old-fashioned looking place in the main street where the proprietor dishes up local food such as *puchero* and *rancho canario* as well as plain grilled fish and steaks. Closed Sat.

Playa del Inglés

Las Cumbres €€ *Avenida de Tirajana 11, tel: 928 760 941*. This long-standing favourite is decorated with old agricultural and domestic utensils. It specializes in dishes from various regions of Spain, particularly slow-roasted lamb, splendid Iberian hams, and prawns from Huelva. Closed May.

Lovin Food €€€ *Avenida de Tirajana 3, tel: 828 991 029,* www.lovinfood.es. Charming hosts Maurizio and Cristina focus on fusion and modern Italian-style cooking at their small restaurant. Each dish is prepared with care and passion and designed to be shared. There are just seven tables so book ahead. Closed Thurs.

Taberna La Caña €€ *Avenida Tenerife 4, tel: 928 761 553, www.tabernalacana. es*. A family-friendly restaurant with a children's menu just a few streets back from the beach. Expect reliably good Mediterranean food, from hearty meals to tapas plates. The paella is a highlight.

Tenderete del Sabor €€ *Avenida de Tirajana 3, tel: 928 968 762, www.tenderetedelsabor.eatbu.com*. On the ground floor of an apartment block, *Tenderete del Sabor* may not look much from the outside, but don't be misled: this unassuming restaurant has served good food for years. Popular with locals, it specializes in Columbian and local dishes. Reservations recommended. Closed Mon.

Puerto de Mogán

La Cofradía €€ *Dársena Exterior s/n, tel: 928 565 321*. A local favourite on the fishermen's quay, where that day's catch comes straight off the boats. Busy and fun at Sunday lunchtime. Try the *cazuela de langosta* (lobster casserole).

Patio Canario € *Urbanizacíon Puerto de Mogán, tel. 928 565 456*. Overlooking the harbour, this friendly restaurant serves fresh fish and local specialities, and is a lovely place to sit and watch the boats. Best value is the catch of the day; grilled and served with vegetables.

Qué tal by Stena €€€€ *Puerto de Mogán, tel: 692 948 986*. This charming haunt only serves a five-course tasting menu, featuring some innovative dishes. Everyone starts at the same time, with an announcement of each dish – some are even prepared in front of customers, which makes for quite the theatrical culinary experience. Open for dinner only.

Puerto Rico

Picasso €€ *Calle Timanfaya 15, tel: 928 560 041*. You'll need to order a taxi for *Picasso* as it's right at the top of the hill. The menu features mainly seafood, fish and steaks, all well prepared and good value. Evenings only.

Restaurante Que Bien €€ *Calle Tasartico, tel: 928 725 963*. With atmospheric lighting and a warm welcome, *Que Bien* makes you feel right at home. The chef often comes up with his own creations, such as ravioli with roasted pork ribs sautéed with honey, parmesan cream cheese and toasted almonds. Plus, the view over the bay is to die for. Closed Wed.

THE WEST AND NORTH

Agaete

La Quisquilla €€€ *Avenida Alfredo Kraus 41, El Turmán, tel: 928 477 696, www.laquisquilla.com*. In the centre of a fishing village, *La Quisquilla* is, unsurprisingly, all about the seafood – and it's excellent; the chef often comes out to check everything is in order. Glass and natural wood give the interior a trendy vibe, and there's a pretty outdoor terrace. Closed Mon–Wed.

Arucas

Casa Brito €€€ *Pasaje Ter 17, tel: 928 622 323, www.casabrito.com*. *Casa Brito* is widely known for its perfectly cooked meats and fresh fish. Of the two rustically inspired dining rooms, the main one has an open wood grill and wood ceilings. Don't miss the home-made guava ice cream. Closed Mon–Tues.

Puerto de las Nieves

Las Nasas €€ *Calle Nuestra Señora de las Nieves 6, tel: 928 898 650*. One of a string of fish restaurants overlooking the port, *Las Nasas* has a cavernous dining room opening out onto a breeze-cooled terrace. Try the signature *ropa vieja* with octopus (*pulpo*). Popular with Las Palmas weekend visitors.

Ragú €€ *Paseo de los Poetas 10, Puerto de las Nieves, tel: 928 886 425, www.ragu.rest*. One of the best seafood restaurants in this little port, serving the likes of octopus salad, fresh fish and shrimps.

Teror

Como Como 15 €€ *Los Viñatigos 15, tel: 639 844 463*. Tucked away from the tourist area, this cosy little restaurant offers a short menu of authentic local dishes cooked to a high standard. The relaxed dining room has a great vibe. Closed Mon–Tues.

THE CENTRE

Artenara

Mirador La Cilla € *Camino la Cilla 9, tel: 609 163 944*. This is the famous cave restaurant, with spectacular views from its sun-bleached terrace, and kitchens cut into the rock. It serves typical, robust meat dishes, many doused in *mojo* sauce.

San Mateo

Casa Martell €€ *Carretera Centro, Madronal, tel: 928 641 283*, www.casamartell.es. In a lovely spot halfway between San Mateo and Santa Brigida, this restaurant can't be missed thanks to its mural-painted facade. Inside, a sprinkling of one-off antiques adds interest to the dining space. Host Antonio is very welcoming and serves up traditional Canarian cuisine that pays homage to the traditions of the island. Closed Mon.

Santa Lucía

El Mirador de Santa Lucia €€€ *Calle Maestro Enrique Hernández, n 5, tel: 928 798 005*. This spacious restaurant serves up hearty local dishes like *salpicón de marisco o garbanzada* (seafood with onions, garlic, tomatoes and peppers) but the biggest draw here is without a doubt the view of the *barranco* (ravine) from the outdoor terrace.

Tejeda

Asador Grill Yolanda €€ *Cruz de Tejeda, tel: 928 666 276*, www.asadoryolanda.com. Next door to *El Refugio*, this is a smaller place that also serves good-value *asados* (roast meats), washed down with fine Canarian wines. A small, covered terrace frames views of Tenerife's El Teide on a clear day. Closes around 8pm, when most visitors have left the area.

El Refugio € *Cruz de Tejeda, tel: 928 666 513*, www.hotelruralelrefugio.com. In the hotel of the same name, *El Refugio* specializes in roast meats, such as goat and rabbit, but its lighter salads are just as tempting. Excellent value and superb views across the mountains. You can eat indoors or on the roof terrace.

TRAVEL ESSENTIALS

PRACTICAL INFORMATION

A	Accessible travel	114	LGBTQ+ travel	124
	Accommodation	114	**M** Maps	124
	Airport	115	Media	124
B	Bicycle hire	115	Money	125
	Budgeting for your trip	116	**O** Opening times	126
			P Police	126
C	Camping	117	Post offices	127
	Car hire	117	Public holidays	127
	Climate	117	**R** Religion	128
	Clothing	118	**T** Taxes	128
	Crime and safety	118	Telephones	128
D	Driving	118	Time zones	129
E	Electricity	120	Tipping	129
	Embassies and consulates	120	Toilets	129
	Emergencies	120	Tourist information	129
G	Getting there	121	Transport	130
H	Health and medical care	122	**V** Visas and entry requirements	131
I	Internet	123	**W** Water	131
L	Language	123	Websites	132

A

ACCESSIBLE TRAVEL

Gando airport and most modern hotels have wheelchair access and facilities for travellers with disabilities, as do the newer museums. For general information, consult the *Able Magazine* (Pentagon Centre, 36–38 Washington Street, Glasgow G3 8AZ; tel: 0141 285 4000, www.ablemagazine.co.uk). Tourism for All (tel: 0845 124 9971, www.tourismforall.org.uk) also provides information for travellers with disabilities. Check the Canary government site (www.grancanariaaccesible.info) for the most up-to-date information.

ACCOMMODATION

Accommodation on Gran Canaria is concentrated mainly in Las Palmas and in large, modern hotels and apartment complexes in the southern resorts. Elsewhere, there is not a great deal of choice. You will struggle to find budget accommodation in the resorts. In Puerto Rico, there are mostly self-catering apartments and aparthotels – where each room has kitchen facilities yet retains all the trappings of a hotel.

Hotels are rated by the Canarian government from one to five stars. Ratings depend largely on facilities; prices within the categories may vary considerably. Breakfast is usually included in the basic rate in resort hotels and larger establishments. Package holidays are most economical, offering accommodation in large, comfortable hotels, usually with swimming pools, and in self-catering apartments. Even if you don't want to spend your holiday in the resorts, they can provide a convenient base. Many hotels have adults-only and/or minimum-stay policies.

There are also apartments and aparthotels, which are typically graded with one to four 'keys' depending on amenities. It is wise to book accommodation in advance, especially during the two high seasons – November to April and July to August.

In the island's interior, there is a smattering of *casas rurales* – rural properties or old townhouses that have been carefully converted into small, medium-priced hotels, or renovated and rented as self-catering accommodation. Contact Gran Canaria Rural (Calle Tenerife 24, Las Palmas; tel: 928 464 464, www.grancanariarural.com).

> I would like a single/ double room **Quisiera una habitación sencilla/doble**
> With/without bathroom and toilet/shower **con/sin baño/ducha**
> What's the rate per night? **¿Cuál es el precio por noche?**
> Is breakfast included? **¿Está incluído el desayuno?**

AIRPORT

Gando airport is located on the east coast, around 20km (12 miles) south of Las Palmas. Bus No. 60 goes to Las Palmas (Parque San Telmo and Parque Santa Catalina terminals) at 15 and 45 minutes past the hour (6.15am–11.15pm). The journey takes around 30 minutes and currently costs €2.30 (San Telmo) and €2.95 (Santa Catalina). There is also an hourly bus (No. 66) to Maspalomas between 7.20am and 8.20pm (journey time 30–40 minutes, costs €4.05), although most visitors going to the resorts will be on package holidays and will be collected at the airport by their tour operator. A taxi from the airport to Las Palmas centre costs about approximately €30.

Gando airport: tel: 913 211 000 (24 hours), www.aena.es.

B

BICYCLE HIRE

Bikes can be hired in the main resorts. A good option is Bike 10Mil, 30 Centro Comercial Gran Chaparral, Playa del Inglés, tel: 663 535 038, www.bike10mil.com. For rental of top-notch mountain and road bikes, try Free Motion, *Sandy Beach Hotel*, Avenida Aleréces Provisionales 6–8, Playa del Inglés, tel: 928 777 479, www.free-motion.com.

BUDGETING FOR YOUR TRIP

Gran Canaria is relatively inexpensive compared with many European destinations. To give you an idea of what to expect, here's a list of some average prices in euros.

Accommodation. Rates for two sharing a double room can range from as low as €60 at a *pensión* or *hostal* to as much as €400 at a top-end five-star hotel. A pleasant three-star hotel will cost in the range of €120–140. Rates drop considerably out of season – May to June and September to October are the least expensive, and are very pleasant months to be there.

Attractions. Most museums charge a small entry fee of €4–5. More expensive are the larger attractions such as Palmitos Park (€32 adults, €23 children); Aqualand (€34 adults, €25 children; both venues are cheaper if you buy online); and Cocodrilo Park (€9.90 adults, €6.90 children).

Buses. Single trips in Las Palmas, €1.40. Buying a rechargeable *bono guagua sin contacto* (pronounced *bono wawa*) cuts the price by around a third. Bus from Playa del Inglés to Las Palmas, around €8 return.

Car hire. Including comprehensive insurance and tax, rates are around €40 a day from the big international companies; you'll snag a better deal if you book for a week. Cars booked in advance online may be considerably cheaper (see Car Hire, opposite).

Getting there. Air fares vary enormously; those from the UK range from £160 up to £600 (€210–790). You'll nab the best deals May to June and September to October. From the US, flights cost around $1000 (€1000). The cheapest flights are usually available online.

Meals and drinks. In a bar, a continental breakfast (fresh orange juice, coffee and toast or croissant) will cost around €5. The cheapest three-course set meal – the *menú del día* – including one drink, will be €8–10. The average price of a three-course à la carte meal, including house wine, will be around €25 per person. At the top restaurants, you may pay double that.

Petrol. Though prices fluctuate, petrol is around €1.20 a litre.

Taxis. Prices are controlled, and reasonable. From the airport to Las Palmas, the fare is around €30. Most trips within the city, and around Playa del Inglés, don't cost more than €7.

C

CAMPING

There are a number of free government-run campsites, called *zonas de acampada*, on the island, usually in attractive and sometimes remote places. You must get a permit from OIAC, Calle Bravo Murillo Las Palmas, tel: 928 219 229, www.cabildo.grancanaria.com.

CAR HIRE (see also Driving)

You must be over 21, sometimes 24, to hire a car, and to have held a driving licence for at least 24 months. You'll need your passport and a credit card. There are dozens of local companies, especially in Playa del Inglés, and these tend to be cheaper. It is also cheaper to hire a car online; CICAR (Canary Islands Car), tel: 928 822 900, www.cicar.com, has been operating for over 30 years. Autos Moreno is a tried-and-tested local company (tel: 928 268 314, www.autos-moreno.es). All the big international companies have offices at the airport, in Las Palmas and in the resorts.

Airport offices: Avis, tel 928 092 330, www.avis.es; Europcar, tel: 911 505 000, www.europcar.es; Budget, tel: 928 092 330, www.budget.es.

I'd like to rent a car for one day/week. **Quisiera alquilar un coche por un día/una semana.**
Please include full insurance. **Haga el favor de incluir el seguro a todo riesgo.**

CLIMATE

In the south, sunshine is practically guaranteed all year round. Winter temperatures average 22–24ºC (72–75˚F), in the summer the mercury rises to 26–28ºC (79–82˚F), though it often tips over 30ºC (86˚F). It can be very windy, even in the hottest months. In the north of the island, temperatures are a few degrees lower and there is more cloud. Higher regions of the mountainous interior are, of course, much cooler. Some rain falls from November to January and in April, but showers are usually short.

CLOTHING

Light summer clothes, sandals and a swimsuit are all you need for much of the time, but bring a sweater or jacket for cooler evenings and for trips to the mountains, and strong shoes if you want to do any walking. A jacket and tie for men and a smart dress for women is appreciated, but not obligatory, in more expensive restaurants. Don't offend local sensibilities by wearing swimwear or skimpy clothing in city streets, museums or churches.

CRIME AND SAFETY

Crime rates are not high, but there is quite a lot of opportunistic bag-snatching and pick-pocketing in tourist areas, especially at markets or fiestas. Robberies from cars are most prevalent, so never leave anything of value in a car. If you have one, use the safe deposit box in your room for valuables, including your passport (carrying a photocopy of your passport is a good idea). Burglaries of holiday apartments occur, too, so keep doors and windows locked when you are out. Report all thefts to the police within 24 hours for your own insurance purposes.

I want to report a theft. **Quiero denunciar un robo.**

D

DRIVING

Driving conditions. The rules are the same as in continental Europe: drive on the right, pass on the left, yield right of way to vehicles coming from your right. Coastal and mountain roads can be extremely sinuous and full of hairpin bends. In rural areas, you may meet a herd of goats, a donkey cart, a large pothole or falling rocks.

Speed limits. 120 km/h (74 mph) on motorways, 100 km/h (62 mph) dual carriageways, 90 km/h (52mph) country roads, 50 km/h (31 mph) in built-up areas and 20 km/h (13mph) in residential areas.
Motorways. Toll-free.
Traffic and parking. In most towns, traffic can be heavy; one-way systems confusing; and road signs inadequate. Early afternoon is a good time to travel into and out of towns, and to find a parking space. It is an offence to park facing the traffic. Don't park on white or yellow lines. Blue lines indicate pay-and-display parking areas.
Petrol. Petrol is much cheaper than in the UK and the rest of Europe, but prices have risen. Unleaded petrol is *sin plomo*. Some larger petrol stations are open 24 hours, and most accept credit cards. In the mountainous centre, there are very few stations.

> **Aparcamiento** Parking
> **Desviación** Detour
> **Obras** Road works
> **Peatones** Pedestrians
> **Peligro** Danger
> **Salida de camiones** Truck exit
> **Senso único** One way
> **¿Se puede aparcar aquí?** Can I park here?
> **Llénelo, por favor.** Fill the tank please.
> **Ha habido un accidente.** There has been an accident

Rules and regulations. Always carry your driving licence with you when you're out in a vehicle. It is a good idea to have a photocopy of your passport with you too. Seat belts are compulsory for all passengers. Children under the age of 10 must travel in the rear of the car. Using mobile phones or GPS devices while driving is illegal.
Traffic police. Armed civil guards (Guardia Civil) patrol the roads on motor-

cycles. In towns, municipal police handle traffic control. If you are fined for a traffic offence, you may have to pay on the spot.

E

ELECTRICITY

220 volts is standard, with continental-style two-pin sockets. Adapters are available in most UK shops and at airports. American 110V appliances need a transformer.

EMBASSIES AND CONSULATES

UK: Calle Luís Morote 6, Las Palmas, tel: 928 262 508.
US: Calle Martínez Escobar 3, Oficina 7, Las Palmas, tel: 928 222 552.
Ireland: Calle León y Castillo 195, Las Palmas, tel: 928 297 728.
South Africa: Calle Albareda 54, Las Palmas, tel: 928 224 975.

If you lose your passport or run into trouble with the authorities or the police, contact your consulate for advice.

Where is the American/British consulate? **¿Dónde está el consulado americano/británico?**

EMERGENCIES (see also Embassies, Health and Police)

General emergencies: 112
National Police: 091

Police! **Policía!**
Help! **Socorro!**
Fire! **Fuego!**
Stop! **Deténgase!**

Local Police: 092
Guardia Civil: 062
Ambulance: 112
Fire Brigade: 112

G

GETTING THERE

By air. There are numerous direct budget airline flights from all UK airports to Gran Canaria. The flight time is 4–4.5 hours. Iberia, the Spanish national carrier (tel: 020 3684 3774, www.iberia.com), now merged with British Airways (www.britishairways.com), flies via Madrid, which obviously takes longer. Check the website and advertisements in Sunday papers for good flight-only deals, but all-in package holidays can be the cheapest way to go.

At present, there are several flights from the US (including New York, Los Angeles and Chicago) operated by British Airways, Iberia and Lufthansa (www.lufthansa.com). Some flights fly via Madrid or Barcelona, or via London airports; check with a travel agency, or visit www.opodo.com. Ryanair (www.ryanair.com), easyJet (www.easyjet.com), Tui (www.tui.co.uk) and Jet2 (www.jet2.com) operate regular flights from London and other British airports.

Inter-island flights are operated by Binter Airlines (tel: 928 327 700, www2.bintercanarias.com).

By ship. Trasmediterránea runs a weekly ferry from Cádiz to Las Palmas, which takes at least two days, and also operates services from Tenerife, Fuerteventura and Lanzarote to Las Palmas. For details, tel: 902 454 645 or visit www.trasmediterranea.es.

The Fred Olsen Shipping Line (tel: 928 290 070, www.fredolsen.es) runs ferries from Gran Canaria to Tenerife six times a day; ships depart from Puerto de las Nieves (near Agaete) and journey time is around 70 minutes. There's a free bus from Parque Santa Catalina in Las Palmas to the ferry terminal.

Naviera Armas (tel: 902 456 500, www.navieraarmas.com) also has regular services to Tenerife, Fuerteventura and Lanzarote. The crossing to Tenerife takes around 2.5 hours.

H

HEALTH AND MEDICAL CARE

Non-EU visitors should always have private medical insurance, and although there are reciprocal arrangements between EU countries, it is advisable for people from member nations to do the same, because not all eventualities are covered. The GHIC card, which entitles UK citizens to free healthcare, is available online at www.gov.uk/global-health-insurance-card. Before being treated, it is essential to establish that the doctor or service is working within the Spanish Health Service, otherwise you will be sent elsewhere. Dental treatment is not available under this reciprocal system. Hotel receptionists or private clinics will recommend dentists.

There are two main hospitals in Las Palmas: **Hospital Insular** (Plaza Dr Pasteur, Avenida Marítima del Sur; tel: 928 444 000) and **Hospital Dr Negrin** (Barranco de la Ballena, just off the GC-23 to the south of the city; tel: 928 450 000). The **Red Cross** (Cruz Roja) is based at Calle León y Castillo 231, Las Palmas, tel: 928 290 000. In the resorts, there are numerous private clinics where you will have to pay for treatment on the spot and reclaim it on your medical insurance. The Las Palmeras chain has clinics in Maspalomas, Playa del Inglés and San Agustín, tel: 928 763 366, www.clinicalaspalmeras.com. In Puerto Rico, the British Medical Clinic (Avenida Tomás Roca Bosch 4; tel: 928 560 016) is reliable. In an emergency, call 112 for an ambulance.

Where's the nearest (all-night) chemist? **¿Dónde está la farmácia (de guardia) más cercana?**
I need a doctor/dentist **Necesito un médico/dentista**
sunburn/sunstroke **quemadura del sol/una insolación**
an upset stomach **molestias de estómago**
Is this service public or private? **¿Es este servicio público o privado?**

Most problems that visitors experience are due to too much sun, too much alcohol or food they are unused to – problems that can often be dealt with by **farmácias** (chemists/drugstores).

Spanish pharmacists are highly trained and can often dispense medicines over the counter that would need a prescription in the UK. They are open during shopping hours; after hours, one in each town remains open all night, the *farmácia de guardia*, and its location is posted in the window of all other *farmácias* and in local newspapers.

I

INTERNET

Numerous hotels, cafés, bars and restaurants across the island offer good internet connections, and many public spaces offer free wi-fi, such as parks, beaches and public transport. In the main resorts, you will find wi-fi with no trouble at all. In terms of consistency, mobile connection is most troublesome in the south around Mogan, Playa de Tauro and Taurito, due to the territory morphology.

L

LANGUAGE

The Spanish spoken in the Canary Islands is slightly different from that of the mainland. For instance, islanders don't lisp when they pronounce the letters c or z. A number of Latin American words and expressions are used. The most common are *guagua* (pronounced *wah-wah*), meaning bus, and *papa* (potato). In tourist areas, basic English, German and some French is spoken, or at least understood.

Do you speak English? **¿Habla usted inglés?**
I don't speak Spanish. **No hablo español.**

The *Rough Guides Spanish Phrasebook* covers most of the situations you may encounter in Spain and the Canary Islands.

LGBTQ+ TRAVEL
Playa del Inglés is very LGBTQ-friendly. The Yumbo Centre is the main spot for bars and clubs, with a vast majority aimed at the gay scene. There's a Gay Pride Festival in mid-May. Visit www.gaymaspalomas.com for more information.

M

MAPS
Most tourist offices will give you free maps, which should be sufficient. For something more detailed, visit the official government bookshop, Librería del Cabildo Insular, Calle Cano 24, Las Palmas, tel: 928 381 539, www.libroscanarios.org. Be aware that many road numbers have changed and the ones on the new maps don't always match those on the road signs.

Do you have a map of the city/island? **¿Tiene un plano de la a ciudad/isla?**

MEDIA
Radio and television. Many hotels have satellite tv with several stations in various languages, including CNN. RTVC is a local station, which includes some English language news and tourist information in its programming. English-language radio stations include Kiss FM Live 102.5 MHz, Power FM 98.2 MHz and UK Away FM 99.9 MHz.

Newspapers and periodicals. Major British and continental newspapers are on sale in the resorts and Las Palmas on the day of publication. A number of English-language publications have island news and tourist information but are not evenly distributed. For Spanish speakers, the island newspapers are *Canarias7* and *La Provincia: Diario de Las Palmas*. Both of these contain listings of events so they can be useful, even if your Spanish is sketchy. *El País* and other Spanish national newspapers are also available.

MONEY

Currency. The monetary unit in the Canary Islands, as throughout Spain, is the euro, abbreviated €.

Bank notes are available in denominations of €500, 200, 100, 50, 20, 10 and 5. The euro is subdivided into 100 cents and there are coins available for €1 and €2 and for 50, 20, 10, 5, 2 and 1 cent.

Currency exchange. Banks are the preferred place to exchange currency but *casas de cambio* also change money, as do some travel agencies, and these stay open outside banking hours. The larger hotels may also change guests' money, at a slightly less advantageous rate. Banks and exchange offices pay less for cash than for travellers' cheques. Always take your passport when you go to change money.

Credit cards. Major international cards are widely recognized, although smaller businesses might prefer cash. Visa/Eurocard/MasterCard are most generally accepted. Credit and debit cards, with a PIN number, are also useful for obtaining euros from ATMs – cash machines – which are to be found in all towns and resorts. They offer the most convenient way of obtaining money and will usually give you the best exchange rate.

Where's the nearest bank/currency exchange office? **¿Dónde está el banco más cercano/la oficina de cambio más cercana?**
I want to change some dollars/pounds. **Quiero cambiar dólares/libres esterlina.**
Do you accept travellers' cheques? **¿Acepta usted cheques de viajero?**
Can I pay with this credit card? **¿Puedo pagar con esta tarjeta de crédito?**

Travellers' cheques. Hotels, shops, restaurants and travel agencies all cash travellers' cheques (albeit there are fewer than there used to be), and so do banks, where you will probably get a better rate. It is safest to cash small amounts at a time, keeping some of your holiday funds in cheques, in the hotel safe.

O

OPENING TIMES

Shops and offices are usually open Monday to Saturday 10am–1.30pm and 5–8.30pm (although some close on Saturday afternoon). Large supermarkets may stay open all day, as do many shops in the tourist resorts, and some also open on Sunday.

Banks usually open Monday to Friday 8.30am–2pm; post offices Monday to Saturday 8.30am–2pm.

P

POLICE

There are three police forces in Gran Canaria, as in the rest of Spain. The green-uniformed Guardia Civil (Civil Guard) is the main force. Each town also has its own Policía Municipal (municipal or local police), whose uniform can vary but is mostly blue and black. The third force, the Cuerpo Nacional de Policía is a national anti-crime unit that sports a dark blue uniform. All police officers are armed. Spanish police are strict, but courteous to foreign visitors.

National Police: 091
Local Police: 092
Guardia Civil: 062

> Where is the nearest police station? **¿Dónde está la comisaría más cercana?**

POST OFFICES

Post offices (www.correos.es) are for mail and telegrams, not telephone calls. The main post office in Las Palmas is at Avenida Primero de Mayo 62; in Playa del Inglés, it is at Edificio Mercurio, Avenida de Tirajana.

Stamps *(sellos)* are also sold at tobacconists *(estanco)* and by most shops selling postcards. Mailboxes are painted yellow. The slot marked *extranjero* is for letters abroad.

> Where is the (nearest) post office? **¿Dónde está la oficina de correos (más cercana)?**
> A stamp for this letter/postcard, please. **Por favor, un sello para esta carta/tarjeta.**

PUBLIC HOLIDAYS

1 January *Año Nuevo* New Year's Day
6 January *Epifanía* Epiphany
1 May *Día del Trabajo* Labour Day
30 May *Día de las Islas Canarias* Canary Islands' Day
May/June *Corpus Christi* Corpus Christi
25 July *Santiago Apóstol* St James' Day
15 August *Asunción* Assumption
12 October *Día de la Hispanidad* Columbus Day
1 November *Todos los Santos* All Saints' Day
6 December *Día de la Constitución* Constitution Day
8 December *Inmaculada Concepción* Immaculate Conception
25/26 December *Navidad* Christmas Day
Movable dates:
Carnaval week of Shrove Tuesday/February or early March, depending on the date of Easter
Jueves Santo Maundy Thursday
Viernes Santo Good Friday

In addition to these, each municipality decides two of its own public holidays, one of which is normally its patron saint's day.

R

RELIGION
The majority religion is Roman Catholic; church attendance is quite high. Respect people's privacy when visiting churches or other religious sites. There are also Anglican, Muslim, Jewish, Mormon and other religious communities.

T

TAXES
The Impuesto Generalisado Indirecto Canario (IGIC) is levied on all bills at a rate of 7 percent. The tax is not usually included in the price you are quoted for hotel rooms.

TELEPHONES
Phone booths accept coins and cards *(tarjetas telefónicas)*, available from tobacconists; instructions in English and area/country codes are displayed clearly. International calls are expensive, so have a plentiful supply of coins or use a card. *Cabinas* – telephone cabins where you make your call then pay at a desk afterwards – are a more convenient way of making long-distance calls. You will find these in Las Palmas (Parque San Telmo bus station, Parque Santa Catalina and elsewhere) and in commercial centres in the resorts.

Calling directly from your hotel room is expensive unless you are using a card from a local long-distance supplier such as at&t or mci. Get the free connection number applicable to Spain from the supplier before you leave (they are different for each country). For international calls, wait for the dial tone, then dial 00, wait for a second tone and dial the country code, area code (minus any initial zero) and the number. Country codes are: UK: 44, Ireland: 353, US and Canada: 1, Australia: 61, New Zealand: 64.

International Operator: 025.

Telephone codes for the Canary Islands (which must always be dialled as part of the number, even for local calls): Gran Canaria, Lanzarote and Fuerteventura: 928; Tenerife, El Hierro, La Gomera and La Palma: 922.

TIME ZONES
The time in the Canaries is the same as in the UK, Greenwich Mean Time, but 1 hour behind the rest of Europe, including Spain, and 5 hours ahead of New York. Like the rest of Europe, the islands adopt summer time (putting the clocks forward by an hour) from the end of March through to the end of September.

TIPPING
A service charge is often included in restaurant bills (*servicio incluido*), so an extra tip is not expected. If it is not included, add around 10 percent, which is also the usual tip for taxi drivers and hairdressers. In bars, customers usually leave a few coins, rounding up the bill. A hotel porter will appreciate €1 for carrying bags to your room; tip hotel maids according to your length of stay.

TOILETS
Toilets in the Canaries are usually called *servicios* or *aseos*. Public conveniences can be found in beach areas and bus stations, and are, for the most part, well maintained. If using lavatories belonging to bars or restaurants, it is considered polite to buy at least a coffee. Some don't ask questions of casual visitors; other proprietors keep the key behind the bar to make sure their toilets are not used by the general public.

Where are the lavatories? **¿Dónde están los servicios?**

TOURIST INFORMATION
Tourist offices abroad
Canada: 2 Bloor Street West, Suite 3402, Toronto, Ontario M4W 3E2, tel: 1-416-961 3131.

Ireland: Callaghan House, 13–16 Dame Street, Dublin 2, tel: 01-6350 200.
UK: 2nd Floor Heron House, 10 Dean Farrar Street, London SW1H 0DX, tel: 020 7317 2011 (no personal callers at office).
US: 60 East 42nd Street, Suite 5300 (53rd Floor), New York, NY 10165-0039, tel: 212 265 8822.
See www.spain.info/en/query/spanish-tourist-offices-abroad for a full list of Spanish tourist offices abroad.

Tourist offices in Gran Canaria
Most towns have a tourist office, open during normal business hours. Some of the main ones are:
Las Palmas: Oficina de Turismo de Gran Canaria, Calle Triana 93, tel: 928 219 600, www.grancanaria.com.
Agaete: Calle Nuestra Señora de las Nieves 1, tel: 928 554 382, www.agaete.es.
Agüimes: Plaza de San Antón s/n, tel: 928 789 980, www.visitaguimes.com.
Arucas: Calle León y Castillo 10, tel: 928 623 136, www.turismoarucas.com.
Gáldar: Calle Plaza de Santiago 1, tel: 928 880 050, www.tourismo.galdar.es.
Maspalomas/Playa de Inglés: Calla Les Dunas 2, tel: 928 723 400, www.turismo.maspalomas.com.
Paseo Marítimo: Centro Comercial Anexo II, tel: 928 768 409.
Puerto de Mogán/Puerto Rico: Avenida de Mogán 1, tel: 928 158 804, www.mogan.es.
San Agustín: Centro Comercial El Portón, tel: 928 769 262, www.turismo.maspalomas.com.
Tejeda: Calle Leocadio Cabrera s/n, tel: 928 666 189, www.tejeda.es.

TRANSPORT

There is no train service, but the bus service is cheap and reliable. In Las Palmas, there are two subterranean terminals, in Parque San Telmo and adjacent to Parque Santa Catalina. Tickets on the *guaguas* (buses) cost €1.40. A rechargeable card *bono guagua sin contacto* is good value for money (€8.50) and can be bought in the bus terminals and in kiosks. City buses run from dawn until 9.30pm, and there's a night service on major routes (tel: 928 305 800, www.guaguas.com).

Long-distance buses leave either from the Parque San Telmo bus station or the Parque Santa Catalina terminal. Buses to the southern resorts are frequent and leave as soon as they are full. They are run by the Global company, which has a centralized information number (tel: 928 252 630, www.guaguasglobal.com). In Playa del Inglés and Maspalomas, services are efficient and run to all the main out-of-town attractions. (For inter-island ferries and flights, see Getting There.)

Taxis. The letters 'sp' (*servicio público*) on the front and rear bumpers of a car indicate that it is a taxi. It may also have a green light in the front windscreen or a green sign indicating '*libre*' when it is free. There is no shortage of taxis in urban areas, and there are usually taxi ranks in the main squares. In towns, the fare is calculated by a meter; for longer, out-of-town journeys there are fixed tariffs, but you may feel happier if you agree an approximate fare in advance. Taxis are good value, with the longest run in Las Palmas costing around €7; from the airport, the fare is around €30. In the southern resorts, where taxis belong to a local co-operative (tel: 928 154 777, www.taxismaspalomas.es), it is also a good, inexpensive way to travel.

V

VISAS AND ENTRY REQUIREMENTS

Most visitors, including citizens of all EU countries, the UK, US, Canada, Ireland, Australia and New Zealand, only need a valid passport. No inoculations are required. Although the islands are part of the EU, there is a restriction on duty free goods that can be brought back to the UK. The allowance is 200 cigarettes, or 50 cigars or 250g tobacco; 1 litre spirits over 22 percent, or 2 litres under 22 percent and 4 litres of wine.

W

WATER

The island suffers from a water shortage, so try not to waste it. It is best to avoid drinking tap water. Bottled water is available everywhere and is inexpensive. *Con gas* is sparkling water, *sin gas* is still. Firgas water, produced in the north of the island, is the nicest.

WEBSITES

You can find a lot of useful information online before you start your holiday. Some helpful sites are:

www.grancanaria.com Oficial de Turismo de Gran Canaria site.
www.spain.info A branch of the official tourist office site.
www.spain-grancanaria.com An excellent general site.
www.hellocanaryislands.com General information site with hotel listings.
For information on natural parks and rural tourism:
www.ecoturismocanarias.com
www.turismorural.com
www.grancanariarural.com

WHERE TO STAY

Accommodation in Gran Canaria can roughly be divided into what you will find in the southern resorts and what is available in the rest of the island. In San Agustín, Playa del Inglés and Maspalomas, you'll mainly find large, modern hotels, and many of these are block-booked by tour companies, although an independent traveller can usually snag a room. Puerto Rico has mostly self-catering apartments and bungalows, many of which must be booked through a travel agent. Puerto de Mogán is unusual in that is does have a small hotel of character, as well as private apartment rentals. In Las Palmas, there is a wide variety of middle- and upper-priced accommodation, much of it near Playa de las Canteras, but good-quality budget digs are harder to find. Outside these areas, rural hotels offer comfortable, medium-priced stays in attractive old buildings.

Each accommodation reviewed in this Guide is accompanied by a price category, based on the cost of two people sharing a standard double room in high season. Breakfast is usually included in hotels in the top three brackets; tax (IGIC) at 5 percent is extra.

€€€€	over 226 euros
€€€	126–225 euros
€€	76–125 euros
€	below 75 euros

LAS PALMAS

AC Hotel Gran Canaria €€€ *Calle Eduardo Benot 3–5, tel: 928 266 100*, www.achotels.marriott.com. This 25-storey hotel, close to Parque Santa Catalina, is set in a striking tower. Ask for a room on an upper floor: you get a great view, the rooftop pool and restaurant are closer, and the traffic noise is less disturbing. Geared more towards business travellers and short city breakers.

Bex Hotel €€€ *Calle León & Castillo 330, tel: 928 971 071*, www.designplus-hotels.com. Boutique bolthole situated in the heart of Las Palmas, with Art Deco-style interiors and an excellent restaurant. The hotel's main calling card, though, is its rooftop bar, where you can linger over a cocktail at sunset while taking in sweeping views of Las Palmas.

Cactus Host € *Calle Dr Miguel Rosas 19, tel: 682 330 179*. Super-clean, tastefully decorated hostel on a boardwalk a short walk from Las Canteras Beach. All the rooms have a flatscreen TV, kitchenette and free wi-fi. The rooftop terrace is a great place to hang out.

Hotel Cristina by Tigotan €€€ *Calle Gomera 6, tel: 203 608 7631*, www.dreamplacehotels.com/en/hotel-cristina. Located right on the beach, the largest hotel in town has all the extras expected of a five-star behemoth, including a large swimming pool, cocktail bar, a string of restaurants and on-site parking. Definitely not the place for those looking for a calm and relaxing break, though.

Hotel Verol € *Calle Sagasta 25, tel: 928 262 104*, www.hotelverol.com. A modern, unassuming hotel situated between Parque Santa Catalina and the beach, filled with 44 clean and comfortable rooms. Good value for money.

Reina Isabel €€€ *Calle Alfredo L. Jones 40, tel: 928 260 100*, www.bullhotels.com. Smartly renovated and with an excellent location on Playa de las Canteras, the *Reina Isabel* is a reliably good place to stay. The highlight is the rooftop swimming pool, and there's a spa with a glass-fronted whirlpool overlooking the sea. The *Summum* restaurant is widely recommended.

Santa Catalina €€€€ *Parque Doramas, Calle León y Castillo 227, tel: 928 243 040*, www.hotelsantacatalina.com. Set in a lush park and founded in 1890, this is the oldest, grandest (and most expensive) hotel in town. Guest rooms are scattered with rare antiques; there's a rooftop bar, a calming spa and a fine restaurant. Staying here is an unforgettable experience, though you'll need deep pockets for the privilege.

Sercotel Parque €€ *Muelle de Las Palmas 2, tel: 928 368 000*, www.sercotelhoteles.com. It might not be the most beautiful of buildings but the interiors have had a revamp, plus you can't beat its central location, right beside Parque San Telmo bus terminal, not far from Vegueta. There is a rooftop restaurant and a choice of good-value rooms and suites.

THE EAST

Agüimes

Escuela Rural Casa de los Camellos €€ *Calle El Progreso 12, tel: 928 785 003*, www.hotelcasaloscamellos.com. An attractive *turismo rural*, with twelve traditionally furnished rooms arranged around a shady courtyard. Run by HECANSA, the Canaries' official hospitality organization, *Casa de los Camellos* has – unsurprisingly – a decent restaurant and bar and friendly, helpful staff. Packed lunches can be made if required.

Santa Brígida

Hotel Escuela Santa Brígida €€ *Calle Real de Coello 2, tel: 928 478 400*, www.hotelescuelasantabrigida.com. Another hotel under the prestigious HECANSA umbrella, *Santa Brígida* offers excellent service and a clutch of spacious, well-equipped rooms. There are pleasant gardens, an outdoor terrace, a gym, sauna and fine restaurant. Close to Las Palmas and to the Bandama Golf Club. Good deals available (Friday and Saturday nights).

Hotel Bandama Golf €€ *Lugar de Golf 14, tel: 928 351 538*, www.bandamagolfhotel.com. Quite small, with just 25 rooms, this is the place for golfers. Tennis and horse riding are also on offer, or guests can just relax in the swimming pool and scenic surrounds. All rooms have either a private terrace or balcony. Special packages for four-day stays with green fees.

THE SOUTH

Maspalomas

Riu Palace Oasis €€€€ *Plaza de las Palmeras 2, tel: 928 769 500*, www.riu.com. One of the most luxurious hotels on the island, *Riu Palace Oasis* is set in a palm grove just a few metres from the dunes. Beautiful gardens, swimming pools, a putting green, tennis courts, billiard room, gym and sauna.

Seaside Grand Hotel Residencia €€€€ *Avenida del Oasis 32, tel: 928 723 100;* www.grand-hotel-residencia.es. This exclusive hotel consists of traditional-style villas and suites tucked away in a lush palm grove 200m from the dunes. It feels gloriously removed from the hubbub of Maspalomas, with attractive tropical gardens and a thalassotherapy centre.

Seaside Palm Beach €€€€ *Avenida del Oasis, tel: 928 721 032*, www.hotel-palm-beach.es. This stylish seven-storey hotel has individually designed rooms, each with its own balcony. Just metres from the beach, with four restaurants, a palm garden and an inviting spa for face and body treatments.

Playa del Inglés

Abora Buenaventura €€€ *Calle Gánigo 6, tel: 928 761 650*, www.lopesan.com. One of the island's biggest hotels, with over 700 rooms, all with balconies. Ten minutes' walk from the centre, but there's a free bus to the beach six times a day. Saying that, you barely need to leave, what with two swimming pools, three restaurants, entertainment including karaoke, a gym, three tennis courts and a wealth of sports activities.

Abora Continental €€ *Avenida de Italia 2, tel: 928 760 033*, www.lopesan.com. Popular with families thanks to a mini-kids' club during school holidays, this all-inclusive hotel also caters to adults with a swimming pool, sauna, solarium and massage treatments, all in manicured gardens.

Bohemia Suites & Spa €€€€ *Avenida Estados Unidos 28, tel: 928 563 400*, www.bohemia-grancanaria.com. Close to the beach, this luxurious adults-only hotel boasts a spa, wellness area, swimming pool, top-floor lounge and a restaurant overlooking the Maspalomas dunes.

Eugenia Victoria €€€ *Avenida de Gran Canaria 26, tel: 928 762 500*, www.bull-hotels.com. Walk through the cool marble foyer to discover spacious rooms, a wellness centre and a restaurant serving up huge breakfasts. There's a large swimming pool and children's entertainment, though the service can feel impersonal. About fifteen minutes' walk to the beach but there's a frequent, free bus. Five-night minimum stay.

Gran Canaria Princess €€ *Avenida de Gran Canaria 18, tel: 928 768 132*, www.princess-hotels.com. This seven-storey hotel, ten minutes' walk from the beach, has spacious, light-filled rooms, each opening onto a private balcony. There's a vast swimming pool, two tennis courts and a sauna. Good out-of-season deals. Adults-only, and two-night minimum stay in summer.

Parque Tropical €€€ *Avenida de Italia 1, tel: 928 774 012*, www.hotelparque-tropical.com. A modern hotel built in a traditional style, with a peaceful location. There's a pleasant garden and swimming pool, tennis courts and a sauna.

Puerto de Mogán

Cordial Mogan Playa €€€ *Avenida de los Marrero, tel: 928 724 100*, www.cordialresortholidays.com. Stunning hotel designed in colonial style, with an esteemed restaurant and a swimming pool set in tropical gardens with an artificial beach, all against a mountainous backdrop. Even the atrium is impressive, with wooden bridges straddling streams and waterfalls.

LIVVO Puerto de Mogán €€€ *Club de Mar, Urb. Puerto de Mogán, tel: 928 099 396*, www.hotelpuertodemogan.com. This pretty little hotel is right on the quayside, so the comfortably furnished rooms have views over the sea, beach or port. Friendly atmosphere, lots of personal touches, a small swimming pool and a pleasant restaurant. The hotel also rents attractive apartments dotted around the harbour, some with roof terraces.

Pensión Eva € *Marinero 65, tel: 928 565 235*. There are few *pensións* on the coast, so this is worth a mention. It's a cheerful little place close to the beach, offering a shared bathroom, communal kitchen and laundry facilities.

San Agustín

Gloria Palace San Agustin Thalasso & Hotel €€ *Calle Las Margaritas s/n, tel: 928 128 500*, www.gloriapalaceth.com. This smart hotel has a poolside bar, tennis courts, mini-golf, a children's playground, a thalassotherapy centre and a welcoming restaurant. About 600m from the beach.

Hotel Dunas Don Gregory €€€ *Calle de las Dalias 11, tel: 928 773 877*, www.hotelesdunas.com. A large modern four-star hotel with all the usual facilities, right by the beach and opposite the shopping centre. All-inclusive terms available.

Paradisus €€€€ *Calle Retama 3, tel: 928 774 090*, www.melia.com. A stunning resort in a prime spot alongside San Agustín Beach. The elegant interior and fine facilities immerse you in luxury. There's a wide selection of room types; pick of the bunch is a sea-view suite with a whirlpool on the balcony. The crop of global restaurants includes an adults-only beach club.

THE WEST AND NORTH

Agaete

Finca Las Longueras €€ *Valle de Agaete, tel: 928 898 145*, www.laslongueras.com. At the bottom of a dirt track off the main road between Agaete and Los Barrazales, this rust-coloured nineteenth-century mansion has been converted into a beautiful *casa rural*. There are nine carefully furnished en-suite rooms and junior suites with great views. Elsewhere, you'll find a small swimming pool and a quiet restaurant serving classic Canarian cuisine.

Occidental Roca Negra €€ *Avenida de Alfredo Kraus 42, tel: 928 898 009*, www.barcelo.com. Built into the volcanic rock, this adults-only hotel is set in a remote spot with panoramic views across the mountains down to the sea, and across to Tenerife. The elegant rooms are spacious and have either a private balcony or outdoor terrace. Extensive facilities include a swimming pool, spa and rooftop restaurant.

Arucas

La Hacienda del Buen Suceso €€€ *Carretera Arucas–Bañaderos Km1, tel: 928 622 390*, www.haciendabuensuceso.com. This rural hotel, in a banana plantation just outside town, is a fine place to relax. It has eighteen rooms, each furnished with antiques and opening onto a private balcony. There is a pretty courtyard and garden, a small heated pool, steam room and whirlpool, a barbecue area and a decent restaurant using lots of local produce.

Gáldar

Hotel Hacienda de Anzo €€ *Calle Pablo Díaz 37, tel: 928 551 655*, www.hotelhaciendadeanzo.es. Cradled in the belly of a valley to the north of Gáldar and close to Sardina beach, this attractive, completely restored country house is nestled among peaceful gardens and has just six guest rooms.

THE CENTRE

Cruz de Tejeda

El Refugio € *Cruz de Tejeda s/n, tel: 928 666 513*, www.hotelruralelrefugio.com. A wonderful place to relax after walking in the Roque Nublo rural park, with a swimming pool and a sauna for tired limbs. Just ten rooms, comfortably furnished, and there's a good restaurant, too.

Parador Hotel de Cruz de Tejeda €€€ *Cruz de Tejeda s/n, tel: 928 012 500*, www.parador.es. Located at one of the highest points on the island, the hotel makes the most of its prime perch with an outdoor terrace framing spectacular views. Wood-beamed rooms have been beautifully refurbished, and the excellent restaurant serves authentic Canarian cuisine.

San Bartolomé de Tirajana

Las Tirajanas €€€€ *Calle Oficial Mayor José Rubio s/n, tel: 928 566 969*, www.hotel-lastirajanas.com. A modern, tastefully decorated, peaceful hotel overlooking the Barranco de Tirajana. There's a heated pool, whirlpool and sauna, a restaurant serving authentic Canarian food, plus splendid views.

Vega de San Mateo

Hotel Rural Las Calas €€€ *Calle El Arenal 36, San Mateo, tel: 655 647 498*, www.hotelrurallascalas.com. Just 3km (2 miles) outside Vega de San Mateo, this intimate hotel offers tranquillity and comfort. Set in lovely grounds, with a kitchen garden that provides fresh vegetables for the restaurant, it has nine individually designed rooms. An excellent base for exploring Tejeda/Roque Nublo.

CASAS RURALES

For a wider selection of rural houses for rent, contact Gran Canaria Rural: www.grancanariarural.com (also see Accommodation, page 114) or www.casitascanarias.com. Price categories given here are per night for two people but are often lower for stays of a week or more. The minimum stay is usually two nights.

€€€ **over 96 euros**
€€ **76–95 euros**
€ **under 75 euros**

Agüimes

Casa de las Suárez €€ *Plaza de Santo Domingo, tel: 928 124 183*. Attractive, traditionally furnished stone house in a pretty square, with solar-heated water, four double bedrooms, two bathrooms and two interior courtyards. No internet, adults only. Seven-night minimum stay.

Casa del Cura €€ *Calle Moral, tel: 928 124 183*. Traditional two-bedroom Canarian house right in the town centre with a private garden.

Moya

Casa Nanita €€ *Camino de la Esperanza 38, Fontanales, tel: 928 464 464*. Three separate self-contained pads in a rural *finca* 9km (5 miles) from Moya, with a swimming pool; lush gardens planted with fruit trees; a barbecue; and bikes.

Teror

Casa Rural Doña Margarita €€ *Calle Padre Cueto 4, tel: 609 751 812*, www.margaritacasarural.com. Opposite the Palacio Episcopal, this tranquil eighteenth-century house shelters four two-bed apartments. There's a roof terrace with sun beds. Tranquil and highly recommended.

APARTMENTS AND BUNGALOWS

Price categories are per night for two people in high season. Only a small selection is given, as many can only be booked through a travel agent:

€€€ **over 96 euros**
€€ **76–95 euros**
€ **under 75 euros**

LAS PALMAS

Bajamar € *Calle Venezuela 34, tel: 928 276 254*, www.hotelapartamentoslaspalmas.com. A couple of blocks back from Las Canteras beach, this modern block shelters four spacious, comfortable apartments, each a different size but all with the essential mod-cons.

Brisamar Canteras €€ *Paseo de las Canteras 49, tel: 928 269 400*, www.brisamarcanteras.com. Strung along the beach, *Brisamar Canteras* has 45 apartments up for grabs; the pick of the bunch have sea-view terraces; guests can make use of the shared gardens.

Colón Playa €€ *Calle Alfredo L. Jones 45, tel: 928 265 954*, www.apartamentoscolonplaya.com. Situated on the sandy shore, many of the 42 studio apartments have a balcony and sea view.

THE SOUTH
Maspalomas

Caybeach Meloneras €€€ *Calle Mar Báltico, Meloneras, tel: 928 14 35 97*, www.caybeach.com. A huddle of fully equipped one- and two-bed apartments, each with a private terrace or balcony decked out with sun beds. Guests can take advantage of an abundance of facilities: three swimming pools (and a splash pool for kids), a wellness centre, gym, mini-golf and a restaurant with pool bar. Located in a peaceful area, but still close to the beach and numerous restaurants.

Eó Suite Hotel Jardín Dorado €€ *Avenida Touroperador Tjaerborg 6, tel: 928 767 950,* www.eohotels.es. This large complex has 114 luxurious bungalows scattered throughout the spacious grounds, as well as swimming pools, a gym and tennis centre. There are special rates at the adjoining golf course.

Maspalomas Oasis Club €€€ *Avenida Air Marín s/n, tel: 928 145 555*, www.maspalomasoasisclub.com. One hundred bungalows are spread across lush gardens, each with basic, clean rooms. There's a swimming pool, tennis courts and children's playground, too.

Playa del Inglés

Bungalows Adonis €€€ *Calle Inglaterra 9, tel: 928 760 785,* www.bungalowsadonis.com. Clean and bright bungalows with large outdoor terraces and private gardens. The complex has a large, shared swimming pool, and is just a short walk from the beach.

Puerto de Mogán

Billy's Venecia Apartments €€ *Urb. Puerto de Mogán, Local 328, tel: 928 565 600,* www.laveneciadecanarias.net. Well-furnished apartments with small terraces and well-equipped kitchens, close to the marina.

Puerto Rico

Apartamentos El Greco €€€ *Calle Doreste y Molina 38, tel: 928 560 356,* www.elgrecopuertorico.com. Attractively designed apartments and bungalows, a stone's throw from the beach, with a restaurant and tennis courts. Mainly booked by tour operators, so may be best to contact a UK travel agent.

Apartamentos Lufesa € *Avenida Tomás Roca Bosch 10, tel: 928 561 225,* www.lufesa.org. A clutch of pleasant apartments in town, so there is no need to climb the hill. Swimming pool, heated in winter.

Apartamentos Mayagüez € *Avenida Lanzarote 22, tel: 928 561 611,* www.apartamentosmayaguez.es. A small complex close to the sea on the Puerto Nuevo side, set in manicured gardens sheltering a swimming pool.

San Agustín

Buganvilla € *Calle Los Jazmines 17, tel: 928 760 300;* www.apartamentosbuganvilla.com. A huddle of modern boutique apartments with views over the beach. Four-night minimum stay.

Sunsuites Carolina €€ *Calle Cardones 3, tel: 928 778 200;* www.sunsuites.es. Pretty whitewashed apartments with private outdoor terraces, a shared swimming pool and lush gardens, close to the beach.

INDEX

A
Agaete 64
Agüimes 47
Andén Verde 61
Arguineguín 54
Aringa 40
Artenara 77
Arucas 70
Ayacata 79

B
Barranco de Agaete 65
Barranco de Fataga 78
Barranco de
  Guayadeque 45
Barranco de Tasarte 58
Barranco de Tasártico 58
Barranco de Veneguera 58

C
Caldera de Bandama 42
Cenobio de Valerón 68
Cruz de Tejeda 76

F
Fataga 79
Finca de Osorio 72
Firgas 71
Fortaleza Grande 81

G
Gáldar 66
  Iglesia de Santiago de
    los Caballeros 67
  Museo y Parque
    Arqueológico
    Cueva Pintada 67
  Poblado y Necrópolis
    de la Guancha 67

I
Ingenio 44

J
Jardín Canario
  Viera y Clavijo 40

L
La Fuente de
  los Azulejos 59
Las Palmas 27
  Auditorio Alfredo
    Kraus 39
  Casa de Colón 33
  Casa-Museo Pérez
    Galdós 29
  Catedral de Santa
    Ana 30
  Centro Atlántico de
    Arte Moderno 33
  El Muelle 37
  Gabinete Literario 29
  La Barra 38
  Las Arenas 40
  Las Coloradas 39
  Muelle Deportivo 35
  Muelle Santa
    Catalina 37
  Museo Canario 32
  Museo Elder 36
  Palacio Regental 31
  Parque Doramas 34
  Parque Santa
    Catalina 35
  Parque San Telmo 28
  Playa de las Canteras 37
  Plaza de Las Ranas 30
  Plaza de Santa Ana 30
  Plazoleta de
    Cairasco 29
  Pueblo Canario 34
  Puerto de la Luz 37
  Vegueta 30

M
Maspalomas 50
  Aqualand 52
  El Faro 52
  El Oasis 52
  La Charca 52
Montaña de Arucas 71
Moya 68

P
Pasito Blanco 54
Pico de las Nieves 80
Pinar de Tamadaba 77
Playa del Inglés 49
Puerto de la Aldea 60
Puerto de las Nieves 63
Puerto de Mogán 55
Puerto Deportivo 55
Puerto Rico 54

R
Reserva Natural Especial
  de Güi-Güi 58
Roque Bentaiga 74, 80

Roque Nublo 74, 76, 79

S

San Agustín 49
San Bartolomé de
    Tirajana 79
San Nicolás de
    Tolentino 60
Santa Lucía 81
Santa María de Guía 68
Sardina 67

T

Tafira Alta 41, 42
Telde 43
    Casa-Museo León
        y Castillo 44
    Iglesia de San Juan
        Bautista 43
Teror 72
    Basílica de Nuestra
        Señora del Pino 72
    Museo de los Patronos
        de la Virgen del
        Pino 73
    Plaza Teresa de Bolívar
        73
Tocodomán 59
    Cactualdea 59

V

Vega de San Mateo 75

THE MINI ROUGH GUIDE TO
GRAN CANARIA

First Edition 2023

Editor: Joanna Reeves
Author: Pam Barrett
Updater: Jackie Staddon
Picture Editor: Tom Smyth
Cartography Update: Katie Bennett
Layout: Pradeep Thapliyal
Head of DTP and Pre-Press: Rebeka Davies
Head of Publishing: Sarah Clark
Photography Credits: Carmencabrera.info 41; Fotolia 71; Gary John Norman/Apa Publications 35; Getty Images 4TC, 4ML, 5T, 6T, 14, 15, 19, 21, 31, 39, 43, 45, 47, 50, 51, 56, 62, 65, 69, 75, 88, 92, 97, 102; Gran Canaria Tourist Board 33, 38, 53, 60, 78, 84, 86; Gran Canaria-info.com 64; Gregory Wrona/Apa Publications 37, 77; iStock 5M, 11, 26, 73, 90, 98; Lucy Johnston 100; Musee Nestor 36; Pam Barrett 70; Public domain 17; Shutterstock 1, 4TC, 4MC, 4MC, 4ML, 4TL, 5M, 6B, 7T, 7B, 23, 24, 28, 48, 55, 58, 59, 66, 76, 81, 82, 95, 104
Cover Credits: Maspalomas dunes R. de Bruijn_Photography/Shutterstock

Distribution

UK, Ireland and Europe: Apa Publications (UK) Ltd; sales@roughguides.com
United States and Canada: Ingram Publisher Services; ips@ingramcontent.com
Australia and New Zealand: Booktopia; retailer@booktopia.com.au
Worldwide: Apa Publications (UK) Ltd; sales@roughguides.com

Special Sales, Content Licensing and CoPublishing
Rough Guides can be purchased in bulk quantities at discounted prices. We can create special editions, personalised jackets and corporate imprints tailored to your needs. sales@roughguides.com; http://roughguides.com

All Rights Reserved
© 2023 Apa Digital AG
License edition © Apa Publications Ltd UK

Printed in Czech Republic

This book was produced using **Typefi** automated publishing software.

No part of this book may be reproduced, stored in a retrieval system or transmitted in any form or means electronic, mechanical, photocopying, recording or otherwise, without prior written permission from Apa Publications.

Contact us
Every effort has been made to provide accurate information in this publication, but changes are inevitable. The publisher cannot be held responsible for any resulting loss, inconvenience or injury sustained by any traveller as a result of information or advice contained in the guide. We would appreciate feedback from readers; please send your comments with the subject line "Rough Guide Mini Gran Canaria Update" to mail@uk.roughguides.com.